SMART RISK MANAGEMENT

A guide to identifying and calibrating business risks

Ron Rael, CPA, CGMA

Chartered Global Management Accountant®

Powered by

14643-349

Notice to Readers

Smart Risk Management: A Guide to Identifying and Calibrating Business Risks does not represent an official position of the American Institute of Certified Public Accountants, and it is distributed with the understanding that the author and the publisher are not rendering legal, accounting, or other professional services in this publication. If legal advice or other expert assistance is required, the services of a competent professional should be sought.

About CGMA

"Two of the world's most prestigious accounting bodies, AICPA and CIMA, have formed a joint-venture to establish the Chartered Global Management Accountant (CGMA) designation to elevate the profession of management accounting. The designation recognises the most talented and committed management accountants with the discipline and skill to drive strong business performance."

About the Author

Ron Rael

Ron Rael, CPA, is a thought leader for the CPA profession on leadership and CFO/controllership topics. He is the CEO of the High Road Institute, a leadership development organization.

Ron has created courses, webcasts, and self-study materials for 12 AICPA courses. He has authored content on topics such as professionalism, customer service, budgeting, accountability, governance, risk management, and strategic planning. A member of the National Speakers Association, Ron has coached more than 10,000 accounting professionals in organisations and leadership teams throughout the United States and Canada.

Ron's industry experience comes from working in two large corporations, as well as from leading accounting teams in numerous closely held businesses. He is a summa cum laude graduate of National University and gained his CPA certification while at KPMG and Moss Adams.

Preface

The goal of your risk management programme is to ensure the continuity of the business and answer this crucial question:

What could disrupt your business model or harm your firm's earnings potential?

Controllers and CFOs must be able to define the payoffs from business risk taking and to explore the methods of understanding, identifying, and reducing the negative effects of everyday business risks. By reading this book, you will define business risk taking and learn to follow a formal process to handle risks better.

This book is designed for any decision maker who recognises that too much effort in controlling risks hurts innovation and not enough control is wasteful and expensive.

After reading this book, you should be able to

- analyse risks.
- discuss how to plan for risks.
- understand how to reduce the potential negative impact of risks.
- understand the 50 risk tools and how to use them.
- help others take risks and be more innovative with less costly downsides.
- see risk taking in an entirely new way.

Contents

Introduction

The Ultimate Risk Taker

Who would you say is the ultimate risk taker? Who is someone you know who takes the sorts of risks you admire?

Keep this person in mind as you read the following story of the person I believe is the ultimate risk taker: Walt Disney.

If you are not familiar with the story of how Disneyland was created, I will recap its history and tell you about Walt Disney. In the 1940s and 1950s, Walt was a film producer in Southern California and usually worked six days per week. On Sundays, he took his two daughters to amusement parks around the area. Although his daughters enjoyed the experience, Walt did not. He and the other parents would sit around with nothing to do while their children were having fun. Most of these amusement parks were dirty, poorly maintained, and sometimes even unsafe.

During this time period, Walt took his family on a tour of the Bavarian Alps and what he saw there really affected him. He fell in love with the castles, the clean cities, and the friendliness of the people. He felt inspired by the Tivoli Gardens in Copenhagen.

These two situations hung around in Walt's creative mind. Soon afterward, he came up with the concept for Disneyland. Like many ultimate risk takers, not everyone immediately buys into their vision, and the same was true for Walt Disney.

When Walt sought financing for his dream of Disneyland, bankers turned him down. He approached other investors who did the same. They asked him questions such as: "Why would anybody want to pay lots of money to go to an upmarket amusement park? Why would anybody want to travel miles into the orange fields of an out-of-the-way place called Anaheim?"

The visionary Walt was tenacious, like all ultimate risk takers, so he persisted in fulfilling his dream. He was approached by ABC Studios to create a children's television programme. Walt agreed to develop one only if it would be willing to finance his concept of an amusement park.

What most people do not know is that Walt ran out of money before Disneyland was fully completed. Several sections were incomplete, Matterhorn Mountain among them. Walt wanted exotic trees all around the park, but ran out of funds before he could purchase them. So he used local trees marked with exotic names—no one noticed!

Disneyland opened as Walt had promised in 1955. Opening day was a fiasco because many things went wrong: rides broke down, they underestimated the amount of visitors, and they ran out of food.

If you look at Disneyland today, however, you can see that it exceeds even Walt's original vision. Disneyland was not "because of a mouse," as Walt was fond of saying; instead, it was built because of his dream, his willingness to take a huge risk, and his tenacity.

We will examine risk in a different way than you are accustomed. Most of us management accountants and financial types think of risk management in one of two ways: either as the concept of risk taking on an individual level or as buying insurance and making sure to have sufficient coverage if a disaster occurs. What you will discover in this book is that risk management is much more. We tend to focus on the small view. My goal is to take you on a journey so that you will understand what true risk management is all about.

This book provides you with 50 different tools to use and 5½ specific steps to follow so that your organisation or client does a better job of managing business risk. The biggest "Aha!" in understanding risk management comes when you embrace the fact that while one side of risk management involves protecting the company from the downside of risk, the other side involves being willing to take that risk.

> *"Oh no! Don't tell me we have to cover that—I hate taking risks!" is what you might be thinking by now.*

You are not really able to be innovative unless you do risk planning. In order to do a good job of leading an organisation, you must look at risk taking and understand what it means on three levels: the individual, the corporate, and the global. You will end up with an understanding of risk from a senior leader's point of view.

Exercise: What Is Your Risk IQ?

Instructions

Complete this self-test to see if you are adequately managing the everyday risks that your firm faces. Place a checkmark next to the questions that you answer with a definite "Yes." Compare the total number of boxes you checked with the answer key at the end.

____   Am I able to sleep at night without worrying about risk in my organisation?

____   Do I have a clear understanding of firm-wide risk, the organisation's key areas of vulnerability, and our ability to recover quickly?

____   Am I confident that an accountable executive is addressing each risk, large and small?

____   Is there a process or function within my organisation that is responsible for assessing, measuring, and monitoring risk?

____   Have we created a realistic balance between innovation and protection?

____   Do our cultural norms help us ensure that all costly risk is identified before we take it?

____   Does my organisation have an operational system or process for evaluating risk?

____   Do I have complete assurance that financial and operational controls are being used as designed?

____   Does my organisation have a thorough and appropriate system with timely reports that use checks or balances on innovation, fraud prevention, and risks faced?

____   Do I have assurance that financial and other information is reported correctly?

___　　Are our processes for risk assessment, management control, and governance being evaluated and reviewed for both efficiency and effectiveness on an ongoing basis?

___　　Is there an emphasis and supporting process within my organisation for aiding productivity and for improving operations?

___　　Are my organisation's stakeholders provided with reliable assurances that its investment is protected by ethical and sustainable means?

___　　If I were not part of the organisation (its management or the board), would I be comfortable with the assurances provided to me as a stakeholder or investor?

___　　Do we have a specific written recovery plan in the event that we suffer from a major risk failure?

Answer Key

13–15 checked—Congratulations!

You have a high Risk IQ! Keep doing what you are doing, and improve those areas you did not check off.

10–12 checked—Good job!

You are effectively managing your risk, but are still vulnerable in many areas. Get started on removing those weaknesses today.

7–9 checked—Scammers love you!

You have so many areas of vulnerability that fixing these vulnerabilities will be like trying to empty a full bathtub with a teaspoon. Get cracking!

0–6 checked—Sharpen your curriculum vitae!

Your company could be out of business within two years.

1

What Risk Management Is and Is Not

Risk management is not simply having adequate insurance.

After reading this chapter, you should

- understand what risk management is truly about.
- understand the 5½ steps of proper risk management.
- be able to get yourself into the correct frame of mind about risk management.
- recognise the importance of being innovative in today's business world and global economy.

Getting Into the Risk Mentality

Exercise: Your Risk

To get you into the correct frame of mind, please write down a specific risk. Think of a risk that your organisation is undertaking or considering:

- What is the risk, both the upside and downside of it?
- Where is the greatest potential for costly risk?
- What makes this venture or activity risky?
- Why are you concerned about it (as the CFO, controller, or auditor)?
- What concerns do others in your organisation have around this particular risk?
- What are the implications or impact on your business or organisation if the risk fails?

Keep referring to this risk as you go through this book. You will be able to understand how the tools work by applying them to your specific risk.

No Insurance Selling Allowed

Whenever this topic is presented to management accountants or other business managers, the first thing they think is: "This person is trying to sell insurance." Having adequate insurance coverage is only one small piece of risk management, as you will soon discover. In fact, in this entire book, only one small section is devoted to insurance coverage.

Risk Is Something CFOs Often Ignore

A survey of 400 leading companies asked: "How prepared are you to protect your revenue drivers in case of a major business disruption?" The survey took the pulse of both risk managers and CFOs.

In the answers, the list of the greatest sources of risk was diverse. Especially telling was how much the risk managers and CFOs differed on the sources. It showed the gaps between how they each defined the management of risk.

The professional risk managers concentrated mostly on property-related risks, whereas the CFOs included improper management, employee practices, and product recalls in their list of greatest threats:

- 100% of the respondents said that a major disruption would have a negative impact on their earnings.
- 28% believe that such a risk would threaten their firms' ability to continue.
- 88% of the CFOs and 83% of the risk managers responded that their company's level or preparation to recover is *less than excellent.*

Anything Can Go Wrong

This is what real world risk management is about: *having a comfort level that whatever risks come your way, you have the ability to deal with them.* This confidence comes from these three factors:

1. Risk management requires having in place a system or methodology to examine risks before you take them—and I stress the word *before.* All too often, accounting and finance departments are consulted about a major risk after the risk has been taken. We are called upon to clean up the mess.
2. Employees have tools to examine and measure the impact of a risk. They know how to use them and apply them in their everyday decision-making efforts.
3. Leaders all across the firm use insightful information to confidently (as opposed to rashly) step into the unknown.

This is the theme of this book, and it will be referred to often:

> *Every risk has a cost. Are you able to pay that cost?*

Process for Implementing an Effective Risk Management Program

Step 1:   Defining what risk is (chapter 4)
Step 2:   Examining your attitude toward risk (chapter 5)
Step 3:   Analysing the firm's ability to handle risk (chapter 6)
Step 4:   Minimising a risk's exposure or downside (chapter 7)
Step 5:   Recovering quickly from the negative effects of a risk (chapter 8)
Step 5½: Learning something so you can accept even more risk with confidence (chapter 9)

Afford the Cost

Now some of you may be already thinking,

> *"But, you are focusing only on the downside of risk. In almost every risk there is an upside. Are you ignoring that?"*

This book was written particularly for management accountants because we often see the downside of risk. Before the upside of risk taking is addressed, consider this question and think seriously as you answer it:

Let us pretend that you just won the lottery today: *"If you won $12 million and were now a multimillionaire, how different would your life be?"*

The following are some typical responses:

- "I will suddenly discover relatives I didn't know I had."
- "Every charity in the world will have my unlisted telephone number on its speed dial."
- "All kinds of people will be asking me for money, even people I do not know."
- "I will have to make serious choices about what I am going to do from now on."
- "I will have to decide if I should work or not."

Most importantly, you will have to decide how your life is going to be different from this day forward.

Do you see the cost for you in winning $12 million?

Most of us would answer: "Yes, having access to $12 million is worth the cost."

This is the price you must consider whenever you buy a lottery ticket. Your costs include losing your anonymity, being in the limelight whether you like it or not, knowing that you will need to be more proactive with your investments, and having to gratefully pay another management accountant to give you financial advice.

Even in the upside of risk taking, costs must be assessed and weighed. This is what risk management is about and why we will most often address the costs and downsides. The tools discussed here will address both sides of the cost/benefit ratio for taking risks.

Analysis of Google's Risk

A *BusinessWeek* article focused on Google and what would happen to it after it decided to go public, in particular, the significant risks the firm faces. A major risk relates to its unique culture. Google currently has an extremely employee-friendly culture; employees enjoy many perks and high pay. Google hires for talent and not for positions. If it finds valuable talent, it hires those people and creates positions for them. The article questions whether that culture can continue in light of competitive pressures and analysts' demands for constant cost cutting.

Another risk is Google's culture of openness. As a public company, the firm will subject itself to the rules public companies face about disclosures, and those rules could affect share prices.

Another major risk is one faced by the two X-gens who started Google, Sergey Brandt and Larry Page. They both have a free-wheeling attitude as risk takers and (according to the article's author) are going to soon find out that they will have significantly more accountability for their actions.

None of Google's risks are good or bad—they just need to be addressed. A question to put before Sergey and Larry is: "In exchange for the millions you generated from going public, are you willing to pay the price of less openness, more accountability to others, and changes to your great company culture?" They would and have answered "yes" (the initial public offering was completed in 2005).

Google's culture will be very different, with less risk taking as time passes. That is part of the cost of being a public and very visible company. The entire leadership team of Google appears, according to journalists who follow Google closely, to have adjusted to the public scrutiny.

One major change in their culture is one predicted long ago as a risk—entitlement. For years, employees were given perks such as free lunches. Now that the costs of these "freebies" are being scrutinised, Google employees feel they are a right and not a privilege. This is causing employee dissension and unhappiness.

Even the simplest things can turn into a risk. This is what risk taking and management is about.

Relationship of Risk and Risk Taking

As shown in figure 1-1, a direct, or one-to-one, correlation exists between taking risks and the amount of the risks undertaken. The more a firm raises the bar or "colours outside the lines" on its reputation and requires employees have a willingness to stretch themselves, the greater the exposures and downsides to the risks taken. Unfortunately, many entrepreneurs and owners of small to medium-sized businesses do not find out about this one-to-one relationship until it is too late. The people who suffer from this expensive wisdom are the firm's employees, investors, and creditors.

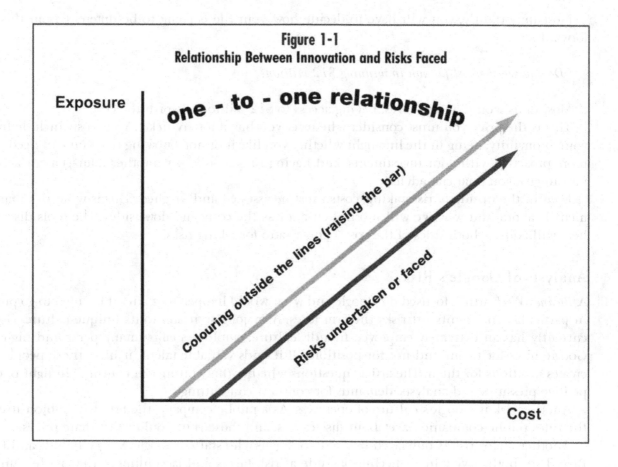

Figure 1-1
Relationship Between Innovation and Risks Faced

Exposure

one - to - one relationship

Colouring outside the lines (raising the bar)

Risks undertaken or faced

Cost

Innovation and Risk Management

Risk taking is fundamental to your firm's ability to create value.

Organisation leaders have an important role in supporting innovation within their organisations. Innovation is defined as a novel way of doing something that is useful. Creativity refers to thinking in novel or new ways, but in today's global economy, creativity is not enough. Innovation—making creativity useable—is required in order to be competitive and maintain long-term strategic advantage.

Today, three kinds of innovations fuel economic growth:

1. Innovations in technology
2. Innovations in business models
3. Innovations in management practices

All three innovation types overlap to an extent, because management practices are the foundation for supporting the first two. In other words, if you have a strong, forward-looking, and strategically aligned management team, your firm will be more likely to have a culture of innovation that is built around a strong and viable business model. Because management practices are critical to innovation, this is where your leaders need to spend their time.

Update the Culture

Making many of today's organisations innovative requires nothing less than an entire revamp of all management practices. The old values of scale, efficiency, automation, and replication are being replaced by an era of imagination, experimentation, and flexibility. These newer values create today's market leaders. The old thinking of caution and careful analysis has been replaced by energy, ideas, and rapid execution. If you doubt this, take a look at those companies that have significantly increased in market value within the last decade: Nestle, AstraZeneca, Tesco, Univision, Cisco Systems, Vodafone, Amazon.com, Tata Steel, Starbucks Coffee, Google, Yahoo, Airbus, Virgin, GlaxoSmithKline, and Compass Group.

Understanding the Innovative and Risk-Taking Organisation

These are traits by which you can identify an innovative organisation. Apply this test to your firm. Do you have

- a compelling vision? _____
- entrepreneurial attitude? _____
- equity compensation? _____
- meritocracy (you earn your place)? _____
- decentralised decision making? _____
- people over policy? _____
- strategic alliances? _____

By putting all these management practices together, you will see that an innovative culture has these cornerstones:

- People are priority number one and are inspired by the big vision to come up with great ideas.
- People are given the support and resources to develop their ideas.
- People are financially rewarded for successful innovation or application of their creativity.
- People are given personal career advancement because of the quality of their ideas.

Survival Creates Infinite Sources of Risk

The world is moving way too fast to have only one set of plans. This is why innovation is not only important but necessary for survival. Today, businesses face a diversity of risks from a variety of sources that are rapidly increasing in magnitude and are driven by the type of business they chose to be in. Whatever the category—such as market, credit, operational, political, or compliance—a question must be asked for each specific risk is: "Is our company exposed to it?" If the answer is yes, the next question must be: "What proactive steps should we take to ease our exposure to that risk?"

There are so many sources of risk today that one could spend a full day just thinking about ways to deal with them. The major sources of risk are detailed in chapter 11, "The Wide World of Risks."

Summary: Risk Is Ordinary and Expected

Risk management is more than just worrying about tomorrow. In today's world, many things can go wrong and put you out of business, *and* if your company is not innovating, it will not survive. These two realities mean that every organisation must have a clearly defined risk management programme that gives its employees tools to anticipate the cost or downside of each risk faced.

2

The Two Views of Risk

What you don't know can kill you.

After reading this chapter, you should

- see risk and its relationship to organisational decision making from the 34,000-foot strategic level.
- see a risk and its relationship to employee decision making from the 100-yard individual level.
- understand why some employees and colleagues are willing to take risks and why others only see risk in terms of black and white.

Duality of Risk

The corporate culture that fosters clever and innovative behaviours and decisions must have two major components of dealing with risk in its risk management programme. One is a global view on the strategic level. The second is a localised analysis of risk on the individual level. If any employee cannot adequately define the risk undertaken before he or she acts, the resulting high costs could damage a firm's reputation. Both views are important and support each other.

Every company must now address the potential impact of unexpected events that could have major financial consequences. Not all organisations have a culture that is prepared for the deep analysis, agile detection, and quick response needed for risk management.

In the book *Best Practices in Planning and Management Reporting*, David Axson, vice president of the Hackett Group, offers three reforecasting approaches that leaders can use to address risk:

- Match your desire for detail with your predictive capability.
- Move toward a forecasting process that balances financial and operational drivers.
- Forecast fewer things more often.

The 34,000-Foot View

Jet pilots rely on sophisticated instruments to "see" where they are going when they cannot see with their eyes. Similarly, because you cannot be everywhere at once, your corporate culture norms and risk management tools allow you to detect costly or painful hazards.

7

Risk Scenario Planning Tool

Running through risk scenarios is one sure-fire method to help leaders understand risk and its likelihood at the 34,000-foot level. Doing so can help establish a clear high to low internal metric that represents the acceptable and unacceptable costs for the organisation. The more your leadership team runs through scenarios, the better it will understand the causes and forces of risk. Important information will be unearthed in these scenario discussions. Of course, your leaders need to include not only financial implications of risks (earnings and cash flow), but also operational implications such as brand, reputation, employment, and oversight of regulators and government agencies.

Exercise: Questions to Gauge Your Risk Tolerance

Determine Your Tolerance Level or the Cost You Can Afford to Lose

Before you undertake the next urgent strategic initiative or action plan, determine the full consequences if you fail to achieve it. Compare the potential losses, including the softer, hard-to-measure ones, against the alleged or expected payoffs.

- *What risk can we afford to take, and what risk can we not afford to take?*
- *When is the risk considered too much for us?*

Measure Your Risk

Adequate risk measurement has two sorts of ROIs; that is, return on investment and return on innovation. There are many different ways to measure these ROIs, but make sure, at set points in time, you know where you are as it relates to the risk you undertake.

- *Why are we undertaking this risk, and why do we believe the payoff exceeds the cost of the risk?*
- *How will we measure this risk to know when to pull the plug?*
- *Who will take responsibility for measuring objectively, and what is that person expected to do with the data?*

Strike a Balance

You cannot be everything to everyone. Stay focused on what you do best, and stick with that as priority number one.

- *What is most important right now?*
- *What have we done best in the past that worked?*
- *What are we trying to become best at in the future?*

The 100-Yard View

Risk taking is an exercise in using creativity.

Far too many employees have the mind-set that they will be punished whenever they stick their neck out or speak out honestly. Change can be implemented more quickly and effectively when people's mind-sets are dealt with before system changes. So, when we discuss managing business risks, we must also explore risk taking. Each employee has a differing view of what is risky and what is not. You need to establish, for the whole company, what a risky activity is and what makes it risky.

Objective Versus Subjective Risk

Each decision made and every action taken in a business setting involves humans. By extension, every risk is entered into by a person. In business, there are two classes of risks: subjective and objective. Risks in the objective class are those for which we can fairly predict a probable outcome in advance. Whenever you toss a coin to decide something, you can predict that 50% of the time the coin will land heads up. There is still a risk that the coin will not show the side you want or need, but statistics prove the 50% odds. People want all their risks to be objective—that is, predictable.

You invest half a million dollars in technology tools but gain no improvements in productivity or cost savings. This risk you took, despite your best efforts, is the class of risk that firms faced most often—subjective risk. It is hard to predict the outcome and even harder to manage. Add in the reality that we all see risks differently, and it is not difficult to understand why proper risk management must include assessing the human factor when analysing risks.

What is risk taking on a personal level? Risk taking is a willingness to face our fears and choosing to do or see something differently.

Personal Risk Spectrum Tool

Consider risk taking on the individual level as a range across a spectrum going from "black and white" on one end to "flying without a net" on the other (see figure 2-1).

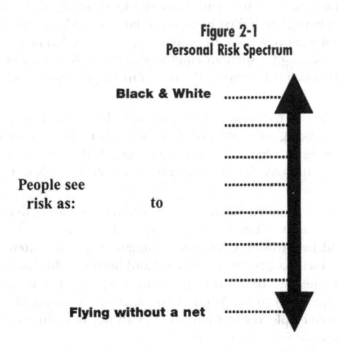

**Figure 2-1
Personal Risk Spectrum**

Example: Personal Risk Spectrum

Raphael is an example of the entrepreneur who has always had an itch to control his own destiny. He retired from a large organisation after 40+ years of placing his career on the black and white side of the risk spectrum. Raphael could not sit still in retirement, so he took some of his pension money and went into self-employment. Raphael found a demand that was not being filled in the industry he knew and loved. His business was quasi-successful until Raphael recognised an even bigger need that had not been met in the moving industry. His new freight-forwarding business grew very fast, and when he needed help, Raphael brought his two daughters into the business with him. In just five years, his business went from zero to grossing over $10 million in revenue. Because of his willingness to risk, Raphael built up a legacy for himself and rewarding careers for his daughters.

True Stories

Some examples to help explain this spectrum:

1. If you want to bungee jump, you could say, "I'm either going to live or I'm going to die." That is the black and white view of risk taking. You might also look at bungee jumping and see only the thrill and exhilaration of the act. You still know that you might get hurt, but instead your focus is on the thrill and excitement of freefalling rather than what you could lose. Your confidence is based on the knowledge that millions of people who have bungee jumped before you have survived. The experience is more important than the cost of what you could lose.

2. In your career, you believe that you have to work or you will be unemployed. So you do not take any risk and do what you must to secure your employment, even though you are not happy in your job. You let being unfulfilled in your job far outweigh the risk or cost of being unemployed. You know jobs are out there in which you could be happier, but you are not willing to pay the cost of looking for such an employer. Security is so important to you that you see it only one way. This way is looking at the risk of unemployment as a black and white issue.

   In your black and white view of risk, however, you are not able to see that alternatives exist, such as working two jobs or being self-employed. You could search for that second job or start a business while maintaining the comfort and security of a full-time job. By doing so, you accept the cost of taking on the risk that if your primary employer finds out, you could end up losing your security blanket.

3. Think of the drive that most entrepreneurs have. They rely on themselves to create a business that fills needs that they see are not being met by others. They often give up the security of a full-time pay cheque and fly without a net into some enterprise. We often read about the successful CEO who started with a $10,000 credit card and built a viable business in the basement. People who live on this end of the risk spectrum accept the risk or cost of not being cautious at times when they need to be. Another cost they see as negligible is surrounding themselves with like-minded employees or friends who will not or cannot be truthful about the foolhardiness of an idea, decision, or venture.

Shanika had a successful and stable career working for a self-development organisation that helps people to grow and become better. After working at this company for many years, she felt that she had done everything she could in her job. Soon after quitting, someone approached Shanika with an idea for a software tool that would help businesses save money. She saw the value of it and borrowed a significant amount of money to develop the idea into a viable product. Despite investing over a quarter million dollars, the business failed. She never imagined the possibility that she could run out of money before the product was ready to market. It happened. Shanika never went back to being an employee, but instead launched a third successful career as a trainer. She continues to fly without a net.

This Spectrum in My Life

For my history, I can look back and see that many times I saw risk taking as black and white.

I considered going up in a hot air balloon or bungee jumping as dangerous undertakings because I have a fear of falling. Then someone gave me a balloon ride as a gift, and during my trip, I realised that my fear was groundless. I have not bungee jumped yet, but I will. Another example is my fear of piloting an airplane. I believe that piloting an airplane could be difficult for me because I am visually oriented, so I must be able to see where I am going. Yet because I fly a lot, I recognise that the pilots often fly using only instruments.

As it relates to my career and employment though, I have been on the fly without a net side of the spectrum. I have always taken risks with my career because I have that entrepreneurial drive.

Although security and providing for my family are important to me, the cost of being on my own is less than the cost of a steady full-time job. Even when I was a full-time employee working for others, I managed a side business or worked part time. At the time I thought I took these risks because of the extra income, but now I realise I needed my freedom and the control of my own destiny.

Individual Risk Taking

Where we fall on the risk taking spectrum boils down to individual values and what we hold dear. We use these intangibles in our cost-benefit ratio of looking at risk. Often, monetary reward is not what drives people to take risks.

Speaking of money's impact on risk taking, if we look at a gambler who risks $10,000 or even $100,000 on the roll of the dice or the outcome of the game, we can see where gambling fits in the risk spectrum. Similarly, look at people who have inherited tremendous wealth and spent it all within a generation. The same varying perspective is true for a person who worked hard to develop her body into that of a competitive athlete and then later let all that hard work and preparation go to waste. Some of us would see that as a waste or loss. Others would say, "She moved on."

In terms of our friends, we slide across the spectrum. Maybe you socialise only with people who have the same beliefs that you do. Or maybe you have friends from all walks of life who, if you put them all in the same room, would find very little in common. With some friends you would discuss only superficial things; however, with others you would tell your innermost secrets.

In addition to sliding across the spectrum, depending on what we hold as risky, people change this view over time. You know of entrepreneurs who in the early days took all kinds of risks to get their businesses started. Then as they grew more successful and mature in decision making, these risk takers began to be more cautious and conservative.

Example: Personal Risk Spectrum

Herman is an example of the entrepreneur who started out his career in the black and white spectrum and over time grew frustrated with his lack of job fulfilment. While working for another company, Herman and another employee saw that their firm was underutilising a product line. The two of them made an offer and, borrowing heavily, purchased that piece of the business. Very quickly they expanded into more markets and have built a very promising and successful business. Yet outside the business setting, Herman and his partner would be seen as cautious and conservative in most aspects of their lives.

Summary: Everyone Sees Risk Differently

As you can see, there are many different flavours in this spectrum of individual risk taking. As a leader who is trying to build a culture that balances innovation with control and develop employees who think for themselves, you must look at risk through the eyes of your employees. This spectrum tool will enable you to do that.

3

Your Firm's Risk Management Plan

You always get what you measure, so measure what you want to know.

After reading this chapter, you should

- understand why a firm needs a defined risk management programme.
- see how to use a risk management plan to help prevent fraud.
- be able to identify who should be the risk champion for an organisation.
- be able to help others foster a risk awareness in an organisation.

Five Stages of Crisis Management

Stage 1: Denial
Stage 2: Containment
Stage 3: Shame mongering
Stage 4: Blood on the floor
Stage 5: Solution

This describes most firms' process for handling risk. In fact most governments follow this process too. Nothing gets better because leaders get stuck at stages 3 and 4.

Your Risk Management Program

Every firm needs a defined risk management program. With one, a firm increases its longevity and profitability. Every day, things occur that could undermine the organisation's success. Wouldn't it be better if an organisation's employees were better prepared to handle those unexpected events?

Assume that a family is on holiday somewhere distant and failed to research the type of weather they might encounter. They might pack for sun, and it turns out to be cold. They might pack for outdoor activities and have to spend the entire holiday inside. This is what a risk management programme is about: matching plans with the existing environment.

In figure 3-1, a global firm-wide risk management programme consists of three prongs or strategies:

1. The first strategy is identification of the specific risks. In this strategy, the goal is to identify and assess risks, measure them, and then use this information to prioritise and strategise each identified risk.

13

2. The second strategy is to arrive at specific ways of dealing with the risk, such as controlling it, mitigating it, or, better yet, avoiding it.

3. The third strategy is to monitor the risk. This is the most neglected strategy of the three because we have to slice and dice each identified risk in four different ways (see figure 3-1). We look at the potential risk at (a) the macro level to determine its effect on the culture, (b) the individual level to see how employees view and handle the risk at the process level, (c) the process level to ensure that firm processes are appropriately considered and, (d) the activity level at which the actual decision takes place.

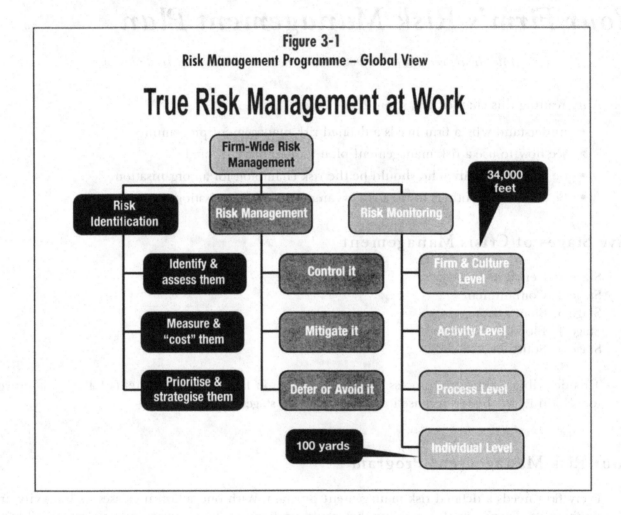

If you have not been involved in a risk management programme, you may notice it looks like a lot of work. It is. However, the payoff is tremendous. This chapter will focus on a few specific areas where you benefit from having a risk management programme, including fraud, financial loss, information, strategy, and business operations.

Fraud and Risk Management

Risk Awareness Prevents Fraud

Almost every business leader believes that only people with high ethical standards work for them. Yet, research shows that fraud is most likely to occur when an employee serves as the sole contact with a particular vendor or when one person performs several incompatible functions. When fraud schemes begin, they are hard to detect and even harder to stop.

There is clear evidence of fraud right in front of you, but you need to know where to look. Awareness begins by

- analysing patterns.
- looking for photocopied or altered forms.
- analysing credit invoices for excessive activity or unusual patterns.
- checking that the vendor was properly approved.
- looking for complaints from outsiders and from employees.
- conducting address checks and site visits more often.

Detecting fraud is difficult even for professional investigators. The best option is to concentrate on prevention. So, having a risk management programme in place forces leaders to seek out areas that are at risk. Areas open to fraudulent activity will be easily uncovered.

Profits and Risk Management

Risk of Financial Loss

A 1999 survey of large companies conducted by Mercer Management Consulting, found that 10% of those companies suffered a 25% or greater loss in shareholder value during a single-month period between June 1993 and May 1998.

The sources of the losses came from

- strategic risk—58% suffered a drop in stock value and traced it back to competitive pressures and revenue shortfalls.
- operational risks—31% of the losses.
- financial risks—11% of the losses.
- hazard risks—no losses were reported because they (usually) had insurance to cover the losses.

This information tells us that other areas are at risk, and that is where leaders need to be watching. These areas can significantly affect an organisation's financial success.

On-Spot Information Gives Rise to Profit Potential

Firm-wide risk management allows organisations to examine all the risks that they potentially face and to measure the impact of those risks on the organisation. Firm-wide risk management also helps firms identify appropriate steps to manage or mitigate those risks. The risks businesses face include, but are not limited to

1. hazard risks, such as property damage and theft;
2. financial risks, such as interest rate and foreign currency exchange;
3. operational risks, such as supply chain problems or cost mismanagement; and
4. strategic risks, such as misaligned products or overaggressive strategies.

The key to your program is to address all those risks in an integrated fashion.

The reason that a risk management programme protects profits is due to the process of identifying, quantifying, and prioritising risks, making them more real and visible to leaders who typically fail to give risk management the attention it deserves. Another reason is that a firm-wide awareness requires a holistic approach to risk management beyond the traditional parameters of things that are insurable. This cultural discipline greatly expands the company's definition of risk to include anything that threatens the organisation's continuity. A company-wide approach helps the firm to sort risks into those that can help the company expand and those that will only lead to loss. In the rush of global competition, sometimes this differentiation is not easy to spot.

The aspect of identifying, quantifying, and managing all the risks that a company could face is compelling but daunting. For any risk management programme to be effective, your organisation must clearly define its goals, make them realistic, and identify their intended results. The end results will both adequately protect the organisation and allow you to identify opportunities to expand and gain shareholder value. Because it would be nearly impossible for the company to quantify every risk it faces, risk identification starts at the 34,000-foot level (see chapter 2, "The Two Views of Risk"). Later in the process, employees will be empowered to deal with risks at the close-up or 100-yard level.

The Risk Champion and Risk Team

Every risk management programme requires a senior-level champion. This champion must be able to assemble a multidisciplinary or cross-functional team that can effectively discuss the risk and the related business issues that the company faces and then share those findings with the entire organisation. Of course, a risk management program must have the support of the board of directors because a risk committee requires representation from all across the company and is necessary to create stronger ties between the oversight of risk and the application of the tools and mitigation of the risks. It will be the ultimate responsibility of line managers—risk takers—to be able to identify, classify, monitor, and control operational risks. Unfortunately, without the risk management programme, most organisations assign their risk management to either a professional risk manager or to their CFO. The champion for risk awareness—the chief risk officer—and the risk team must take the time to understand why the company has succeeded in the past and is currently succeeding or not succeeding.

The biggest challenge of a risk management programme is to bring the company to a point at which it can identify the risks that are the greatest threat to its continued expansion and success, quantify the size of those risks, and, then, take steps to manage or mitigate them. Although most businesses with risk management programmes initially identify between 50 to 100 or more specific risks, the key is to narrow it down to the top 5 or 10 risks that are significant enough to warrant quantifying and analysing. Once a company has identified its key risks, it has to quantify the magnitude of those risks. Quantification helps the leaders to decide whether to control, prevent, finance, insure, or avoid the risk altogether.

In the event that a risk needs insurance, your company still needs to take a fresh approach. While adopting specialised insurance approaches, your organisation needs to work toward long-term solutions. For example, a risk to your firm's brand might be easily mitigated currently, but over time it could have a significant negative impact on the marketplace if not addressed today. Brand risk is an example of an exposure that may not be covered by your current insurance coverage. This is why your recovery plan is critical to the successful implementation of risk management. Throughout the entire risk management process, companies must retain a strategic focus. This is another reason why a senior-level executive must be the champion of your risk management efforts.

Your Business Plan Risk

A company's business model is made up of two components:

1. The organisational structure and processes
2. The impact on operational risk from decisions made

In addition, if an organisation is unable to perform or execute its strategy, the firm incurs execution risk. To assess and measure execution risk, a company focuses on the results it generates from the structure of its marketplace and its business model. Within the theory of your business model, three specific global risks reside:

1. Strategic risk
2. Operational risk
3. Innovation risk

Strategic Risk

Strategic risk is defined as the inability to align with competitive pressures and customer sufficiency. Falling under the threat that you cannot carry out your strategy are eight risk categories:

1. Operational risks (execution of your strategy and goals)
2. Reputation risks (impact on your reputation and brand)
3. Financial risks
4. Hazard risks
5. E-commerce and technology risks
6. Intellectual capital risks
7. Ethical risks
8. Integrity risks

Risky Strategy Leads to Ethical Risk

Strategic planning is managing change and overcoming risks. It is a critical process through which risks can and need to be identified and dealt with in advance.

For your firm to manage your strategy risk, the leaders must develop acceptable expectations for all products or services. A risk to your firm's ethical standards is involved in this process, because there is intense pressure on the organisation and the employees to meet a lofty goal, to achieve its business plan, and to satisfy creditors or investors. The more this pressure is applied, the more likely people will undertake unwarranted risk. If these wild, out-of-control leaps fail or do not achieve the high expectations, there is urgency for people to cover them up. Thus, your integrity is at risk.

Risky Market Leads to Integrity Risk

In market risk, firm integrity is involved and can be damaged when your research or studies are flawed or when your assumption of the customer's needs is skewed in favour of the organisation. Many market studies have been accepted as true without consideration of the realities of the marketplace or not obtaining true customer buy-in. Facing this risk requires you to get your input about the competitive environment from the source.

Risky Capability Leads to Integrity Risk

The capability or internal risk is another place where extreme pressure is felt when it is clear you will not achieve your goals. It is important to challenge people's ability and to test their capability to expand and improve. However, leader hubris combined with undue pressure often manifests when you over-promised and must now under-deliver. People will want to massage the numbers, to make up data, and of course, to hide the internal faults. This last trait leads to buck-passing and blaming. These behaviours, of course, negatively affect the profits and damage integrity. The net result is bad news for all.

Operational Risk

Operational risk management looks at the business from the operation itself and is defined as the risk of direct or indirect loss resulting from inadequate internal control, processes, people, and systems to react to external events. Financial information is not enough to gauge a company's overall business risk.

The value of managing operational risk is only slowly gaining recognition. One reason is that by the time the financial impact of management's misjudgement affects the balance sheet or income statement, it is typically too late to do anything about it other than pick up the pieces. By tracking operational indicators and metrics, leaders can identify opportunities and threats *before* they affect the company's finances.

One approach to measuring operational risk requires firms to routinely review many nonfinancial factors such as the quality of corporate governance, employee morale, customer satisfaction, implementation of goals and execution of those goals, the company's application of technology, and its deployment of those practices. Numerous tools that enable you to easily measure operational risk already exist, such as the balanced scorecard, activity-based costing, or driver-based forecasting.

Budgeting Hampers Operational Risk Identification

Most companies still rely on planning and budgeting process and reporting techniques that may have been created decades ago. To improve the likelihood of detecting operational risk, organisations can do the following:

- Update their technology
- Use advanced analysis tools
- Apply for ISO 9000
- Use a balanced scorecard reporting system
- Incorporate activity based costing
- Invest in an enterprise-wide accounting system

Managing operational risk requires a systematic, objective, and comprehensive framework that assesses all of the nonfinancial variables that could contribute to an organisation's risk portfolio.

All firms incur certain operational risk simply when choosing their marketplace and its customer base. Business complexity and revenue volatility are directly affected by the structure of the market. Technology, regulations, the consumer, and the global economy all drive changes in market structure. All of these must be factored into the assessment and valuation of your operational risk.

Key Drivers of Operational Risk in Your Market Structure

- Number of participants
- Degree of concentration
- Level of regulation
- Competitive environment
- Rate of business expansion
- Capital intensity
- Barriers to entry
- Product life cycles
- Availability of alternative markets
- Risk of obsolescence

Key Drivers of Risk in Your Business Model

- Governance model
- Organisational structure
- Product or service delivery model
- Process complexity
- Technology complexity
- Sourcing strategy
- Best practices utilisation
- Management discipline
- Staffing and employee skills
- Leadership competency

Key Drivers of Risk in Your Execution Efficiency

- Revenues
- Earnings
- Cycle times
- Expansion
- Quality
- Service levels
- Productivity
- Market position or market share
- Management competency

Key to Measuring Operational Risk

The starting point to measuring operational risk is to make sure you are collecting the right data. This requires a complete and balanced view of your important business metrics across at least three dimensions and must include a mix of leading and lagging indicators. Your operational data must be able to describe how a core operation is conducted within your organisation.

To overcome any information deficiency, your organisation must effectively combine operational and financial data in order to form a more complete and timely picture of operational risk, while decreasing your reliance on historical financial reports. Your leaders need to assemble a list of possible and predictive metrics for the business and then test them to make sure that they correlate the time lag of the activity indicator to the time of its financial impact. The ultimate payoff is that you can use these operational risk metrics as targets for your budgeting process. Thus, your budgeting process strengthens.

Regularly assessing your firm's operational risk profile benefits the shareholders. Of course, leaders and the employees of the organisation develop their ability to both spot and manage risks and, most importantly, convert them into opportunities. Understanding your risk profile is a benefit to your customers and suppliers as well. This insight gives your leaders clues into areas that offer the best benefit for allocating resources and making tough decisions.

Effective operational risk management has gone from an "I would like to do" attitude to a "We must do this" frame of mind.

Innovation Risk

Companies undertake three sources of risks when they believe they are innovative and desire a culture in which employees think for themselves. In a culture of innovation and creativity

- Innovation Risk Source No. 1 is the strategy risk. This requires clear direction setting and involvement to help the entire organisation know where it is going and have the ability to measure progress.
- Innovation Risk Source No. 2 is market risk. This is the fear that the company fails to be in touch with the customer's needs and demands.
- Innovation Risk Source No. 3 is capability risk. This is a fear that the company will not be able to execute carefully designed plans and use the innovation to generate revenues.

Practical Solutions for Managing Business Model Risk

Strategy

The solution to making your firm less vulnerable is for your leaders to clearly define each of the firm's risks though your risk management programme. It is particularly important to identify strategy risks early. This involves a matching of the role or purpose of your innovation with a specific strategic need for each new and existing initiative. Without such guidelines, new products, new ideas, and new services will misfire.

Market

For market risk, you need to prevent the risk that the innovation will not meet your market's needs. You need to ensure that you differentiate yourself from your competition or position yourself differently from what everybody else is doing. Because market risk is more difficult to measure and monitor, companies usually end up paying less attention to this risk. The number one reason for new product failure today is the inability to compete in both global and local marketplaces.

Operations

Minimising operational risk, such as insufficient internal capability to deliver what you promised, or that your new product will not be developed within the desired time and budget, requires foresight and honest self-assessments. Defining your innovation risk up front will allow you to take the critical first step toward successfully managing it.

Innovation

All too often, leaders' expectations for new products go largely unspoken. They are in someone's mind, but frequently not communicated adequately to others. Most importantly of all, there is no way to measure innovation and creativity. To help manage this risk more effectively, you need to develop and explicitly publish agreed upon expectations for any and all of your innovations. This process involves coordination of three separate and related tactics that allow you to effectively gauge how much risk you can afford to take.

10½ Rules for Successful Business Risk Taking

1. Focus on trouble, and you will get trouble. Focus on success, and you will get success.
2. Trust that your people know what a risk is.
3. Recognise that your people may not know how to recover from the negative effects of a risk.
4. No risk is worth undertaking when proper planning or analysing cannot be completed beforehand.
5. No risk is worth undertaking when a "lessons learned" cannot be completed afterwards.
6. Every plan of action and strategy must have a feedback instrument built into it.
7. Understand the costs of your risk tolerance and your risk avoidance.
8. No one is exempt from making errors in judgement.

9. Tell the truth about the risk and its implications. Accept the truth about the risk and its implications.

10. Be willing to live with the negative results of each risk undertaken.

10½. Want more rewards? Take more risks. Want more success? Reward risk taking.

Answer this question:

What are these rules telling you about risk and risk taking?

Summary: Risk Requires a Proactive Plan

Global perils can come from any place within the business model, your strategy, or a new marketplace. Each one can deeply affect your firm's

- profits,
- creativity,
- continuity,
- brand or reputation,
- leaders' integrity,
- employees' ethics,
- internal capabilities, and
- goal execution.

This is why the firm-wide plan for anticipating and dealing with these risks must become part of your everyday managing and leading.

4

Step One—Define Risk

The first step is always the hardest.

After reading this chapter, you should

- be able to test your definition of what risk is with others.
- understand why the company's leaders must establish the corporate definition of *what is risk* every year.
- recognise the limitations of trying to purchase insurance to cover every risk.

There is a saying that goes, "Talking about bulls is not the same as being in the bull ring." Therefore, we must grab the bull by the horns and face the situation. This, in essence, is step 1.

Exercise: Defining Risk

1. Write down the phrases or terminology you would use to define the word *risk*.

   Risk is ...

2. Write down the phrases or terminology you would use to define *risk taking*.

   Risk taking is ...

3. Next, ask a friend or colleague to define his or her definition of risk and compare your definitions. You will see that there is some terminology that is similar and some that is different. Write down any similarities you see.

The point of this exercise is to demonstrate that there are numerous ways for people and professionals to see and define risk.

The goal is to jump-start the process of gaining a consensus on a commonly acceptable definition of what is risky and what is the cost we cannot afford.

How others define *risk* (the most common answers): *Risk is ...*

- "Doing something different."
- "Going outside my comfort zone."
- "Scary."
- "Worth the effort."

23

- "Something that has an upside and a downside."
- "Putting something valuable on the line that I could lose."
- "The unknown or X-factor."
- "Where I could get hurt or harmed."
- "A goal or destination that may not be achievable but is worth trying for."
- "A means to an end—hopefully rewarding or beneficial."
- "A movement forward despite any downside."
- "A gamble."

How others define *risk taking* (the most common answers): *Risk taking is* ...

- "Going into the unknown."
- "Doing something proactive."
- "Having to face up to a potential loss or gain."
- "Going for something that has a payoff and a possible downside."
- "Doing a cost benefit ratio and proceeding with the assumption that the benefit is higher."
- "Putting something valuable at risk, often things other than money."
- "Taking a chance."
- "Pushing the envelope on what may not be acceptable."
- "Scary or frightening."
- "Not taking a chance."
- "Striving for some prize that may not be easy or even attainable."
- "Gambling."

Taking the First Step

What is required in step 1 of your risk management programme is for the leaders and critical decision makers of your company to sit down once a year and examine risk. At this off-site meeting, they dispassionately define, for the organisation, what is considered risk taking and what costs they cannot afford. Over the life of the organisation, this definition will change dramatically.

What You Will Discover in Step 1

By going through this exercise of examining different people's views of both risk and risk taking, you will discover a wide variety of definitions. The opinions will range from the optimistic to the pessimistic. Some will focus on the upside or payoff (*worth the effort*) and others will focus on the downside or pain (*where I could get hurt or harmed*). Others will give you a balanced response, such as: "*Something that has an upside and a downside.*"

When you compare all the various answers, you will see a trend of three to five similar responses. Do not get caught up on the specific wording; instead, focus on the message behind the words. Your goal in step 1 is to get the group to arrive at a consensus on a mutually acceptable definition for both risk and risk taking. The consensus will almost always be the balanced view. It is amazing how pessimistic management accountants tend to be when discussing risk. Likewise, it is never surprising when marketing staff and executives see risk as something necessary as they look through rose-coloured glasses.

If your organisation fails to take this first critical step in implementing a risk management programme, you will find that employees will take on more or fewer risks than they should. Employees will focus only on either the upside or downside of a risk. Some employees will ignore or overlook activities or decisions that contain risk, while others will exaggerate the odds of failure.

Why Defining Risk Is Necessary

Boards of directors and other stakeholders of companies are more wary of risk than ever. To ensure their own job security, CEOs must become more aware of the need to develop more sophisticated means to measure and manage everyday business risks. Numerous experts agree that there is far less tolerance by stakeholders (especially in public organisations) for the executives who fail to prepare for a disaster of some sort. This leaves boards, shareholders, and executives searching for broader and better ways to manage risk in order to achieve their goals and ensure strategy viability. Thus, the entire organisation must focus on the causes of risk instead of the traditional method of treating only the symptoms or focusing on the protection through insurance.

Operational risk management, as defined earlier, is managing the risk of loss resulting from three sources:

- Inadequate or failed processes or systems
- Human factors
- External events

Operational risk management requires clearly defined authority and accountability for each sort of identified risk.

Practical Solutions for Making People Aware That Risk Exists

Simple Solution One
Share best practices across your organisation. For this to occur, your culture must be one of openness, with managers as co-dependent partners within the risk environment. This partnership must include employees from the operational side of the business and employees, whose advice is typically ignored such as the audit, finance, human resource, and risk management teams.

Simple Solution Two
Implement a governance structure. This is an integral part of the firm's operational risk programme. Governance promotes cultural transparency and openness together with demanding accountability from each employee, each operating unit, and every support function.

Simple Solution Three
Identify, collect, and monitor a balanced set of critical performance indicators or metrics that help the leaders to identify control issues and allow for early mitigation. This solution is also important to operational risk management.

Case Study Analysis of a Bank's Evolving Risk Appetite

Started as a regional bank, Bank went from a button-down institution to an aggressive lender in the land and buildings marketplace.

In 2003, Bank entered into a now infamous area known as subprime lending. Investing in the subprime market is controversial, among other reasons, because of the risks it poses for lenders due to the low quality of the debt and the higher interest rates that the buyers pay. However, Bank believed that it could earn better margins in the subprime business because of its efficiency.

In 2009 Bank acquired a major credit card provider, Credit Card, a once-troubled lender that bounced back from the brink of failure to become a prime takeover target. The combined company would have gross income of over $12 billion. With most of its profits tied to home lending, Bank counted on credit cards to diversify its revenue. Bank planned to use Credit Card as a springboard into the credit card industry. Bank's executives believed profits could rise even higher if the two companies successfully sold more products to each other's customers.

Bank was preparing to launch its own credit card before concluding it made more sense to buy the expertise and existing customer base of a major lender like Credit Card. The CEOs of both companies are risk takers. Credit Card's management team engineered a dramatic turnaround as the company battled to survive heavy losses that piled up from the company's former specialty of issuing credit cards to risky borrowers. Credit Card's prior management team took on a risk that failed; the new team took one that succeeded.

Ultimately, the risks Bank undertook, focusing solely on the upside of higher than average returns and rapid expansion, have come back to undermine its finances and reputation and the value of its stock has suffered substantially.

Answer this question:

Do you understand why your leaders need to review risk annually?

Insurance's Inadequacy in Risk Management

Every day insurers are finding different exposures that they had not encountered before. The major stumbling block with insurers is the lack of historical data. Insurance companies use history to determine both the size of the risk and its statistical probability. From this data, the insurer sets a rate to charge its clients. This information must be reliable and always arrives years after the risk is identified.

For example, your business model requires a heavy dependency on a contract manufacturer. You are unaware that the contract manufacturer also consults with your competitor, causing your business harm. They failed to disclose this to you. When you discover this conflict of interest, you have to find and engage another contractor. You ask your insurance company for compensation, and they ask you, "What are your economic losses?" You are unable to show specific out-of-pocket costs other than some travel and legal fees. You argue for the loss of face to your customers and damage to your reputation for the effort in having to scramble to find an alternative supplier and for lost future earnings. But because this is a contractual relationship and one not addressed in your policy, chances are that your insurance company will not reimburse you beyond your out-of-pocket costs.

The phenomenal expansion in electronic business or e-commerce is another major and hard-to-quantify risk in business today. Although awareness to this risk is rising, some insurance companies still have a hard time getting senior insurance executives to recognise that this exposure requires a new strategy or approach.

Uninsurable E-Commerce Risk

All companies that pursue a business based around technology need to rethink their risk management processes. For example, when a software application in use becomes critical to your business and when organisations undertake business-to-business integration, risk increases significantly. Your risk exposure builds because your partners can connect to your core data system. The exposure also builds because your critical applications are operating 24/7, which increases the likelihood that someone may tamper with your systems. A disruption in business due to a virus or an electrical blackout could significantly affect your firm's financial performance. The potential losses associated with system malfunctions can manifest in multiple ways, such as the loss of income due to business interruption, investor reaction that hurts share price, and the loss of trust in the integrity and reliability of your information system and website.

For the business that relies heavily on technology, effective insurance policies must underwrite losses according to the decline in economic value of damaged property, whether it is proprietary information or intellectual property. As more losses include intellectual property thefts, companies need to ensure they have adequate internal protections. A core part of your risk management programme needs to address intellectual property issues. Knowledgeable workers with access to a company's proprietary information may not know that they are misusing that information.

Uninsurable Risk of Doing Business Across the Globe

Another difficult to quantify, yet uninsurable risk, is doing business globally. Even though you may not invest in facilities in a foreign country but are simply building a distribution channel or a base of operations to provide business services, you must closely examine the inherent risks associated with those activities. Be sure to develop specific cost-effective plans to address exposures, such as regulatory compliance, indemnity, currency, commodity price fluctuations, and employee or contractor safety.

What it All Means

No matter what new business risks are on the horizon or ones that have yet to have a label applied to them, a business leader's main concern needs to be:

> *How do we adequately overcome these risks with our own risk management programme,*
> *especially when insurance coverage is inadequate or unavailable?*

Fostering Risk Awareness Case Studies

Analysis of a Financial Company's Lack of Risk Awareness

Financial Co. took a very large risk that came back to haunt it. In one year alone, the company lost more than 500 million pre-tax dollars—and its top executives were initially clueless about how it happened.

In 1997, Financial Co. began investing in risky high-yield junk bonds and other similar securities far more heavily than its competitors and higher than industry norms. As investments began to turn sour, both the CEO and the CFO did not have a handle on the problem (risk) nor the amount of the losses. The company failed to identify a risk management officer, which means that no one was responsible for reviewing the portfolio of risk for the company's investments.

Financial Co.'s drive to invest in these junk bonds was a result of the extreme pressure the company put on managers to increase earnings. Despite having a successful financial advisory business, Finance had nearly exhausted the profits it could make from that venture. The advisory business was not growing fast enough to generate the top-down mandated profits.

An executive decision was made to increase the company's investment mix as a result of the tremendous pressure being applied by Finance's chairman, who demanded a return on equity growth of 15% an aggressive amount for the industry. Finance's investment arm decided to raise its junk bond portfolio to from 8% of its $25 billion investment pool to 13%.

About the same time, another executive, who headed the high-yield investments, recommended that the firm go one step beyond junk bond investments and invest in the growing market for sophisticated financial instruments called Collateralised Debt Obligations (CDOs), which offered interest rates of 20% or greater. Collateralised debt is supposed to spread the risk by tying together a large number of securities. At the time, CDO issuers were buying up the low-grade bonds of cable, telecommunications, and healthcare companies, among others. They would package this shaky debt into new securities for sale. Even though the underlying bonds carried junk ratings, each new CDO was supposed to offer investors a portfolio with a broad range of risk.

These high interest rates attracted Finance's attention. With huge sums of money in its coffers from the insurance and annuities premium paid by its customers, Finance jumped into the CDO marketplace. Within three years, all junk bond prices tumbled, causing some CDOs to be hit with downgrades at the same time that Finance's junk bond portfolio was bombarded with defaults.

In the end, Finance's entire high-yield investment portfolio deteriorated rapidly, and, because many different parts of the organisation were acting independently of one another, no central employee or executive saw the disastrous big picture. Executives had been relying largely on reports generated by an outside CDO manager to evaluate the health and performance of Finance's investment portfolio. It was not until a few senior executives sat down with Finance's entire portfolio along with an in-house analyst that they saw the full picture regarding the company's entire portfolio exposure.

Finance was able to recover from this fiasco. The lesson here is that this typically conservative business was under extreme pressure by its chairman to increase earnings. Empowered employees were able to enter aggressively into a high-risk exposure without the corresponding controls, checks and balances, or reporting mechanism to ensure that risk was carefully managed. The cost that Finance could not afford was the loss of some key personnel, the public embarrassment, the billion dollar loss, and the 29% hit on its firm value.

Risk Awareness Tool

The Institute of Internal Auditors (IIA), an international professional association, is a useful resource for information and tools to deal with the downsides of risk. Although its primary mission is to support the internal audit community, internal auditors are becoming a valuable member of the risk management team. For large companies, the internal auditor regularly examines operational areas where risks are likely to occur.

One of IIA's tools is the following questionnaire aimed at leaders, executives, and board members to create awareness for them regarding risk. As you go through the questionnaire, see how many of these you can answer "yes" to. Each "no" answer is something you need to be more concerned about.

- Is there a process or function within the organisation responsible for assessing and monitoring risk?
- Do I have assurance that controls are operating as planned?
- Is there a thorough and appropriate reporting mechanism within the organisation that allows for adequate checks and balances for fraud prevention and risk management?
- Do I have assurance that financial and other information is reported correctly?
- Are risk management, control, and governance processes being evaluated and reviewed for efficiency and effectiveness on an ongoing basis?
- Do I have a clear understanding of enterprise-wide risk and the organisation's key areas of vulnerability?
- Does the organisation have an operational system for managing risk?
- Is there an internal process within the organisation for adding value to and improving operations?

- Are the organisation's stakeholders provided with reliable assurances that their investment is protected?
- If I were not a part of management or the board, would I be comfortable with the assurances provided to me as a stakeholder?
- Am I able to sleep at night without worrying about risk in the organisation?
- Am I comfortable that all risks have been appropriately addressed?

Source: The Institute of Internal Auditors and the *Journal of Accountancy*, January 2000.

Summary: Importance of Step 1

Step 1 of an effective risk management programme is necessary to ensure that every decision maker in your organisation is in agreement about "colouring outside the lines." As you will discover in the next step, there are many different views of what is risky and what is not. Without a common or mutually accepted view of risk, employees may effectively have a blank cheque.

Because accountability is very important to successfully running an organisation and ensuring that internal controls prevent unwarranted or illegal behaviours, your carefully crafted and thoughtful definition allows executives to create a standard and expectation. This accountability helps to ensure that your firm maintains the delicate balance between being innovative and rash risk taking. This is not an easy step to take, but it strengthens your organisation's ability to deal with whatever unforeseen risk you may encounter.

5

Step Two—Examine Attitudes Toward Risks

After reading this chapter, you should

- be able to implement step 2 of your risk management plan.
- understand your own attitude toward risk taking.
- understand the uncertainty domino.
- see how the risk taking entrepreneur views risk.
- understand the motivation for someone who avoids taking risk.

Exercise: Determine Your Risk Tolerance

Exercise No. 1

Please answer these questions:

Do you take risks? Yes ___ No ___

How do you know that you do or do not take risks?

Is it because other people tell you that you do or do not?

Is your answer because of your definition of risk?

Exercise No. 2

Take this quick self-test by answering "yes" or "no." These five simple questions will give you an assessment of your risk inventory.

Yes	No	Question
		Do you sometimes have endless debates with yourself when you have to make an important decision—sometimes making no decision at all?
		Do you accept poor service from a waiter or clerk rather than speak up?
		Do you have a hard time making an emotional commitment to others?
		Do you find excuses to stop yourself from getting a better job, learning new skills, or taking advantage of similar opportunities for self-improvement?
		Do you let the disapproval of others keep you from doing things you want to do?

31

Any "yes" responses indicates that you probably shirk from taking significant risks. I know that some people may not like hearing that. However, in reality, there are many differing attitudes toward risks. Some people would do things that other people would not.

Exercise No. 3

Which of these activities would you define as risky?

_____   Driving a race car at more than 200 miles an hour

_____   Flying commercially once a week

_____   Mountaineering

_____   Deep sea fishing

_____   Driving fast on a busy road

_____   Having children

_____   Pursuing a university education

Each of these activities will be considered risky by some, not risky by others. For example, many people may consider having a child or two not to be risky, but may find five or ten children more risk than they can tolerate. And then there are people who do not get married because the thought of having even one child is just too risky. Likewise, a university education can carry a high cost in both money and effort, and at the same time choosing the wrong field of study can lead to underemployment or unemployment.

Your daily trips to and from work may carry a greater risk than you driving on a race track at 200 miles per hour. But which of these activities do you consider more risky?

The Second Step

Risk is all about how you view something.

By now you should be convinced that people have differing attitudes toward risk taking. The basis for taking step 2 in your risk management programme is to understand and acknowledge this. This impact is felt at the organisational level.

> Let us examine risk management principles 1 and 2:
>
> • People do not take risks because of fear.
> • Risk taking is a necessity for individual and business success in this changing world.

Now we will return to the individual, or 100-yard view of risk.

Personal Risks

There are three major personal risks that we all fear and face:

1. Self-improvement risk:
   You wish to enrich your life for the better, yet self-improvement holds the possibility of *failure*.

2. Commitment risk:
   You define yourself by the commitments you make, yet commitment holds the possibility of a *wrong choice*.

3. Self-disclosure risk:
   You must be honest with yourself (in other words, your feelings, your concerns, and so on) before you can disclose yourself to others, yet self-disclosure holds the possibility of *rejection* and *humiliation.*

The Uncertainty Domino

When it comes to understanding how we look at risk, the uncertainty domino helps (figure 5-1). Every domino tile contains two numbers. You can play the number on one side of the domino, or you can play the other number, so you always have two options. Similarly, people can look at risk in two ways: as a problem or as an opportunity.

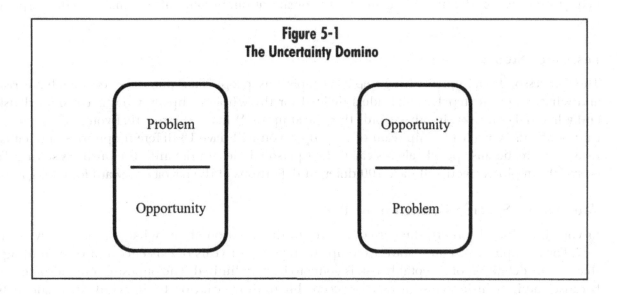

**Figure 5-1
The Uncertainty Domino**

Most of us in management accounting and finance see risk as a problem. We understand what cost is, we know the dire implications of risk failure, and our own fears come into play. We see a risk as a problem because that little voice in our brain says, "I don't think we should be doing this."

There are just as many in the world who consider activities such as rock climbing or scuba diving as great opportunities. They would define the choice as "a chance to try something new" or as "a thrilling experience."

> This leads us to risk management principle 3:
>
> • Risk taking is in the eye of the beholder.

Motivation Behind Avoiding Risk

Why do we take so few risks, especially with our money?

The fear of loss is the motivator for seeking gains. We can find losing money so distasteful that it blinds us to seeing risk as an opportunity to gain something. However, the elation that comes with winning is short term compared to the feelings of shame and regret we hold onto whenever we lose. Our feelings of loss are much stronger than our drive for a gain. Similarly, failure in our past can sabotage our willingness or confidence to take a risk. This affects our belief that we can succeed again. This adopted attitude, at its worst, means that we will take no risk at all. Risk averse people tend to magnify the consequences of failure to the point that we lose sight of the upside. We must not let that happen if we choose to succeed.

While this has been a discussion of the individual view of risk, it also applies to an organisation, because every team, company, and agency is made up of people. How we act as an individual is how we act as a group. Our fear of loss must not become an acceptable excuse to making progress or being innovative for the individual and for the organisation. Individual egos make up the corporate ego.

Lesson of Step 2

The core lesson from implementing step 2 is simply this: people have differing views of what is risky and what is not. In step 1, your leaders defined for the whole company what is considered risky and what makes it risky. In other words they faced up to "What is the cost that you as the company cannot afford?" On a leadership team of 13 people, you will have 13 different opinions of what is a risky venture, because people always carry their personal view of risk into the business setting. For every 100 employees, you will have 100 different definitions of the payoff or reward for taking a risk.

Your Firm's Specific Definition of Risk

In your firm, like all others, the correct answer to the question about what is a risky activity can vary. For example, if you are a start-up company in your first years of existence and your funding is shaky, your definition of acceptable risk is going to be very limited. The opposite could also be true. Because you have little to lose, it may be acceptable to throw caution to the wind. Many successful firms started out this way, such as Apple and Microsoft.

If your company is well established and has survived at least 15 years, the definition of risk will be much broader and wider. Your leaders may decide that growing by 150% in one year is too risky, but growing incrementally at 30% per year is an acceptable risk.

What if your company is a multibillion dollar international conglomerate? Your leaders' definition of risk is going to be extremely different than the start-ups' definition.

During recessions, many companies hunker down, cut expenses, and strive to weather the storm. Other organisations use such difficult periods as an opportunity to go on merger or acquisition sprees, to spend more on research and development, to invest in new products or new customers, or to create new channels.

If you face a major economic downturn, ask yourself the following questions:

Does your firm have a strategy to

a) hunker down and take little risk, or

b) take a risk such as growth, acquisition, or investment in the future?

Outsourcing as a Risk

Other farsighted organisations have used recessions as an opportunity to streamline their operations and decide which functions to outsource.

Answer these questions:

Do you see outsourcing parts of your business operations as a risk or as an opportunity?

Why do you see outsourcing this way?

Do the executives of your firm see outsourcing as something you should or should not do?

Have they ever considered outsourcing?

Exercise: Taking a Risk

Think of a major risk you have taken in your life, either personal or business related.

Tell a friend or colleague about this risk. Explain what you learned from this experience and, all things being equal, whether you would do it again.

Write down the major risk _____

_____

_____

_____

_____

Would you consider yourself to be a risk taker? Does your friend or colleague consider you to be a risk taker?

Which of the major personal risks did this activity explore (from the "Personal Risks" section in this chapter)?

What made this a risky activity?

How does this relate to the topic of managing risks?

The point of this activity is to show that while you may not define yourself as a risk taker, the person listening to your risk may look at it as something risky. Likewise, you might describe what you did as taking a risk, but the person you describe it to may not see it as a big risk taking adventure. It all boils down to how each individual person views risk and in finding the value or danger of any particular venture into the unknown.

The Mind-Set of the Risk Taking Entrepreneur

Call it a genetic compulsion, a defensive reaction, or simple optimism, but the reality is that most business owners refuse to contemplate the possibility of failure. It is as if the word does not exist in their vocabulary. However, failure is an option. The downside of this "never say die" attitude is that it can be ruinous, wasteful, costly, and hurtful, and it can spoil opportunities for future success.

Most entrepreneurs see themselves as the types of people who put their heads down and charge full steam ahead. However you can badly injure yourself with that mind-set. This person does not avoid risk, but he or she ignores it at every opportunity. This person fails to recognise that failure is an option. This is why risk can be mismanaged or unacknowledged.

Considering the possibility of failure in risk taking, there is a very delicate line to walk. It is better to assume failure can occur than to resign yourself to it. It is acceptable to acknowledge our fear but not let ourselves to be overcome by it. Walking that line requires courage.

The Mind-Set of the Risk Averse Person

Even though many industries prize and value people who take risks, there is a group of people who tend to be risk averse. We often describe this group as those "stuck in the mud" management accountants.

Often, we say that we should take more risk because we see how risk taking is revered in our culture. Just look at the honours bestowed on Olympic athletes and poker players amongst others. However, when reality sets in, and we realise that we could actually lose money, others will see the type of risk takers we really are. Generally, people *hate* to lose money. *People hate to look stupid or incompetent.*

Back to Us

People in finance and accounting own the mentality, "I am the guardian of the assets," and this attitude leads us to look at risk differently.

When making a critical decision, taking risk is composed of the following:

- How emotional versus how rational I am
- How confident versus how anxious I am
- How impulsive versus how reflective I am

Risk is inherent in nearly all facets of business, including expansion, mergers, research, and contraction. Therefore, no matter how much a decision is researched, we, as management accountants, must face that uncertainty will always exist in any strategy and decision.

A controller or CFO wants to make sure that they do not do anything stupid. But that is very different from taking a risk. The controller or CFO's job is to put forth the best alternative, suggest the pros and cons, identify the opportunities sought, and then show what the future could look like in both scenarios. While doing this evaluation of a risky situation, we must keep an eye on potential gains or upsides as well as potential losses or costs.

Case Study

Analysis of Royal Bank of Canada Revisited Risk Definition

Royal Bank of Canada recently found that privacy was its primary risk and turned that knowledge into an opportunity. The bank's privacy policy is centred on retaining and enhancing customers' trust, which has become an integral part of the bank's overall strategy and everyday business practices. This meant that the bank needed to move to a higher level of privacy beyond meeting the minimum regulatory requirements.

Based upon customer feedback through research, the bank discovered that 83% of its customers would close their accounts if they felt their information was being used inappropriately or was not being protected. Leaders recognised the tightrope they walked—protect the customer's information or use that information to provide better service. They recognised the need for acceptable balance. Therefore Royal Bank of Canada altered its strategy toward risk taking to the following: "Everything we do, every process we develop, has the customer balance at its root."

A 10½ Step Plan to Build Your Self-Confidence for Risking

1. Understand your tolerance level for risk
2. Recall that you have risked successfully many times before
3. Deal with your anxiety for risk taking first
4. Emphasise the reward or risk instead of the risk or reward ratio
5. Make decisions with less data to build your intuition
6. Do not overplay the significance or downside of the risk by asking: "What is really my cost?"
7. Rely on your intuition—it is usually right
8. Get the counsel of a risk taker you admire
9. Know that the cultural norms always affect individual risk taking
10. Know that you always have choices, no matter the initial outcome
10½. Remember that not all risking is risk taking

Answer this question:
What are these rules telling you about encouraging people to see risk differently?

10½ Rules of Creative Risk Taking

1. All risk taking involves a choice.
2. All risk taking requires an investment.
3. All risk taking can fail.
4. Risk takers put themselves and their egos on the line.
5. All risk taking is accompanied by feelings of stretching or rising to the challenge.
6. All risk taking requires facing our anxieties:

   a. Humiliation

   b. Failure

   c. Wrong choice

   d. Rejection

7. All risk taking carries important psychological rewards.
8. Virtually all risk taking sparks feelings of excitement, novelty, movement, and change.
9. Every risk taker remembers experiences of prior risks taken.
10. Risk taking is not gambling.
10½. Take risks—or die!

Answer this question:

What are these rules telling you about risk management in a business?

Exercise: Who Is Running the Train?

Instructions

In the table that follows, think of five areas in which your organisation often faces or takes risks. List them. Next, enter the name of the person who is responsible for managing the area at risk. Last, think about that person's individual approach to risk taking.

Spectrum of Attitudes Toward Risk Taking:

Flying Without a Net   **Black and White**

Aggressive	Assertive	Middle of the Road	Conservative	Very Conservative

Risk Area	Person Managing This Risk	Person's Attitude Toward Risk Taking
1.		
2.		
3.		
4.		
5.		

Answer these questions:

What did you notice about the prevailing attitudes toward risk taking in the people that are "running the train" in your firm?

Is the attitude of the person managing your risk area appropriate, too much, or inadequate?

Is there a balanced view in your organisation?

Summary: Importance of Step 2

If your firm fails to take step 2, and immediately proceeds to step 3, *your risk management programme may fail*. Your management team, like all others, is made up of different individual mind-sets toward risk taking and the cost of failure. If these individual mind-sets are not addressed openly, action plans and strategies will lack balance. This delicate balance between being innovative and protecting ourselves is critical to having an effective risk management plan.

We must not let the "cost-conscious, bean-counter" mentality slow down our need to innovate. We cannot let the "there is unlimited possibility" mentality foster unwarranted risk and reckless decision making. Step 2 emphasises the need for both views of risk as a catalyst for achieving ever greater success.

"If you refuse to take chances, you are stuck, which today is taking a step backwards."

Step Three—Analyse the Firm's Ability to Handle Risk

After reading this chapter, you should be able to

- describe to others the impact that corporate culture has on risk management.
- look for specific risks in an organisation's critical strategies.
- describe, from a self-assessment, the level of accountability that people display in your organisation.
- describe for others how the three budgets, the operating plan, and the financing plan are used in managing risk.
- apply the risk-by-identification tool to analyse a specific risk.
- use the ideas in this chapter to foster a culture that balances risk taking with risk exposure.

Case Study

Analysis of Amazon's Ability to Take Risks

Another example of an ultimate risk taker is Jeff Bezos, the founder and CEO of Amazon.com. Jeff is confident that his organisation can take big risks and survive. For example, Amazon ventured into the furniture business, even though that proved to be unfeasible at first. Today, Amazon uses its website as a pull-through for vendors such as Art.com. Jeff's company started the Z stores, and now that risk brings tremendous revenues without much cost. Jeff and his team continue to foster relationships with other organisations, such as Toys "R" Us and Martha Stewart Living. Some of these partnerships have succeeded and some have flamed out, but Amazon continues to take big risks within the framework of its business model.

Back in 1997, so-called experts predicted that with the launch of BarnesandNoble.com, Amazon was going to soon be "Amazon.toast," but Amazon thrived and expanded. As 2000 approached, Amazon's share price fell from $100 to $6, but Jeff did not see this as failure. Amazon posted its first real profits in 2003 and was on track to exceed $11 billion in sales, growing at an annualised 16%. Meanwhile, as of February 2006, the stock was at $39 a share, giving it a market value of nearly $17 billion. Amazon, eBay, and a few others have endured as the survivors of the Internet Age, using the lessons learned from the "dotbombs" to build successful organisations with viable business models.

As of early December, 2011, Amazon stock was selling for a little under $200 per share.

Jeff credits his legendary luck to creative innovation. He uses farsighted thinking and relies on his intuition. Yet he is also a "by the numbers" boss who prefers to measure everything using spreadsheets. He bases most of his critical decisions on this data, not judgement or instinct, and uses numbered lists for all things that he needs to do. What separates Jeff from his less successful colleagues are his nightmarish (to some) leaps of faith. His best decisions cannot be backed up by studies or spreadsheets. He makes nervy gambles on ideas that to outsiders seem too big or too audacious and not bottom-line oriented. Jeff introduced innovations that initially hurt Amazon's sales and profits for the short run, yet turned out to be the right decisions. They increased customers, which in turn increased profits. The culture that Jeff has created is adept at coming up with innovations. Yet he employs best practices to learn from other successful businesses and from competitors.

Jeff is described as the rare leader who gets excited over finding small improvements and efficiencies within Amazon's operations, while maintaining a grand vision of a changing world. He is both stubborn and flexible at the same time.

Another example of Jeff's thinking is to go against the prevailing generally accepted notion that good communication is important. Jeff believes "communication is terrible." He adopted within Amazon the concept of the "two-pizza team," which means that if you cannot feed a team on two pizzas, then the team has too many members. It is within Amazon's two-pizza teams that their innovation is fostered. These teams create some of the quirkiest and most popular features on the Amazon site. Jeff is constantly testing the marketplace and taking large risks to see if his intuition pays off. Sometimes it works and sometimes it does not.

To summarise, by relying on the numbers, his team's best instincts and judgements, and his instincts, Jeff practices effective risk management. He is willing to take large risks while understanding their cost. At the same time, he knows that his risks can be wasteful, and he makes sure that he has confidence both in the numbers and his people.

Case Studies to Learn From

To help you understand how step 3 works, we will explore two risk taking companies, Discount Store and Clothes for Men. You will have information on both companies, highlighting the specific strategies each one uses to stay successful.

Exercise: Risk Analysis

Instructions

Select one of the two companies. Your goal is to select a specific strategy of that organisation and write down as many risk exposures to the strategy that you see. Assume that you are an investor or on the board of directors of your selected company, and you are presented this new strategy. It is your responsibility to critique it. You can be hypercritical. Look at the strategy and list all your concerns. Be sure that you can justify your concerns to someone so that you refrain from basing your analysis on your personal fears.

Case No. 1—How Risky Is Discount Store's Strategy?

Read the following summary of Discount's strategy. Select one or two strategies Discount employs to retain its advantage. List the potential risks Discount faces with each strategy in the following chart.

<u>Discount's Strategy Element</u>   <u>Discount's Risk Exposure(s)</u>

Discount's Strategy for Competitive Advantage

Discount's Business Strategies. Goal: To reinforce its reputation for high quality products at low prices by

1. creating merchandise excitement.
2. growing private label offerings.
3. introducing cross-marketing opportunities with other businesses.
4. maintaining well-run facilities and operating efficiencies.
5. monitoring price savings on all items and leverage over suppliers.

Discount's strategy is based on the concept of offering customers very low prices on a limited selection of nationally branded and selected private label products in a wide range of merchandise categories. This produces rapid inventory turnover and high sales volumes. When combined with the operating efficiencies achieved by volume purchasing, efficient distribution, and reduced handling of merchandise in no-frills, self-service warehouse facilities, Discount is able to operate profitably at significantly lower gross margins than traditional wholesalers, retailers, and supermarkets.

Case No. 2—How Risky Is Clothes for Men's Strategy?

Read the following summary of Clothes for Men's strategy. Select one or two strategies that Clothes for Men employs to retain its advantage. List the potential risks Clothes for Men faces with each strategy in the chart that follows.

<u>Clothes for Men's Strategy Element</u>   <u>Clothes for Men's Risk Exposure(s)</u>

Clothes for Men: Success in a Declining Industry
Clothes for Men's Global Business Strategy.

1. The company positions itself as a high quality, yet lower price, store of choice for men's business clothing.

2. They target the up-and-coming professional who has a need for a sharp and polished look but can't necessarily afford high-end labels.
3. The selection of clothing is limited and changes several times a year to keep up with current trends.
4. They sell the lesser quality products of well-known brands.
5. The stores are located in the shadow of their direct competition.
6. The rental of men's wedding wear is a major profit centre.

The company's leadership emphasizing treating its employees as well as it expects them to treat customers.

The Point

The lesson in this activity is that a critical piece of any reality-based planning process is to examine the risks associated with each strategy in your business plan. The source of risk in every business organisation comes from one place, which will be explained further later in the chapter, and the person who promulgates that risk is usually the founder, CEO, president, or the significant decision maker.

Risk of Weak Accountability

Take this single self-test on accountability and be as honest as possible.

After you have completed for yourself and your organisation, read the answer key in the exercise that follows to understand the risk that currently exists within your organisation.

Exercise: Accountability Self-Assessment

Instructions

Rate your company (or department) on each item to determine how well your firm or team displays accountability. Be brutally honest!

This is how my boss acts:

He or she rarely does what he or she says he or she will do.			He or she usually follows through.		His or her words and actions always agree.	
1	2	3	4	5	6	7

This is how we follow through on our commitments to one another:

We ignore one another's needs.			We try to support one another.		Every person feels supported.	
1	2	3	4	5	6	7

This is how we follow through on our commitments to outsiders:

We laugh when they ask for help.			We often deliver what we promise.		Outsiders are always pleased.	
1	2	3	4	5	6	7

This is how we hold each other responsible when someone does not follow through:

The person gets away with it.			Sometimes the person is talked to.		Follow-up is immediate.	
1	2	3	4	5	6	7

This is what happens when something goes wrong:

The focus is on who goofed.			We blame and the fix the problem.		We focus on how to prevent it again.	
1	2	3	4	5	6	7

Answer this question:

Because the 6 and 7 scores show maximum accountability, what does this tell you about the level of accountability that exists within your company?

Answer Key

If you rated your organisation or your boss as "1" or "2" then you are not being honest or *you need to work for a new company.* If you rated your organisation or your boss as "6" or "7," then you are also not being honest because you have a narrow view of the situation.

More realistically, in each of the five scenarios you would have rated your firm or team between 3 and 5.

Why? Because accountability is an attitude and a choice, and just like every choice, some days we feel like making the choice, and some days we do not. It is impossible for anyone to be accountable every moment of the day. Things occur and events happen in which we suddenly and immediately play the blame card, or we make a commitment and then forget about it or fail to follow through. Real life happens. What I want you to examine in the self-assessment is the overall attitude within your organisation that people have toward accountability.

The Point

The lesson in this activity is that accountability is the cornerstone for a balanced risk management plan. If people refuse to act in an accountable manner, they will shirk their responsibilities for reducing unnecessary or costly risk.

What happens if the executive or the board is asleep at the wheel and they are not concerned about risk? You have Kmart, Oasis Hong Kong Airlines, Woolworths Group, or Merck; the list grows every day.

Therefore, as management accountants, we must understand that the major source of your firm's risk is the impact that leaders play in coming up with and implementing a strategy. This is why including a proper risk management programme is a must!

Now let us turn to this source of almost all business risk: your strategic plan.

Answer this question:

What is strategic planning?

The Source of All Business Risks

Strategic planning is managing change and overcoming risks. Strategic planning is a process through which risk can be identified and dealt with. Figure 6-1 outlines a sample flowchart for strategic planning.

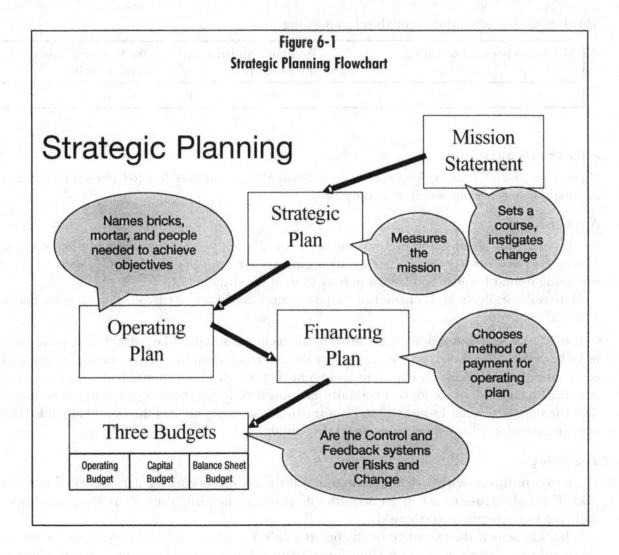

Figure 6-1
Strategic Planning Flowchart

Strategic planning starts with your mission statement because it sets the organisation on a course and instigates change—from today's status quo to where we want to be in the future.

The second element of strategic planning is your actual strategic plan, the measurement of your mission. In this document you identify specific metrics and methods of measuring whether or not you are accomplishing your mission over the next 18–24 months.

Information from the strategic plan flows into the operating plan, which identifies the technology, facilities, and people you need to achieve each specific objective in your strategic plan. The operating plan is where we are headed and what we will commit to accomplishing in the next 12 months.

Out of your operating plan comes your financing plan. In this document you highlight the methods of payment for the technology, facilities, and people in your operating plan. For instance, how much capital will come from internal sources and profits? Will some of the funds come from outside investors? Will additional funding be required from banks or other lenders? These are the questions that get answered in the financing plan.

Finally, from the financing plan, you develop your budgets: the operating budget, the capital budget, and the balance sheet budget. These three documents become your control and feedback systems over the risks and the changes that you started with your mission and strategy. This is a holistic look at your planning continuum that reminds us: "We really need to plan carefully." An overview of a risk management programme is outlined in figure 6-2.

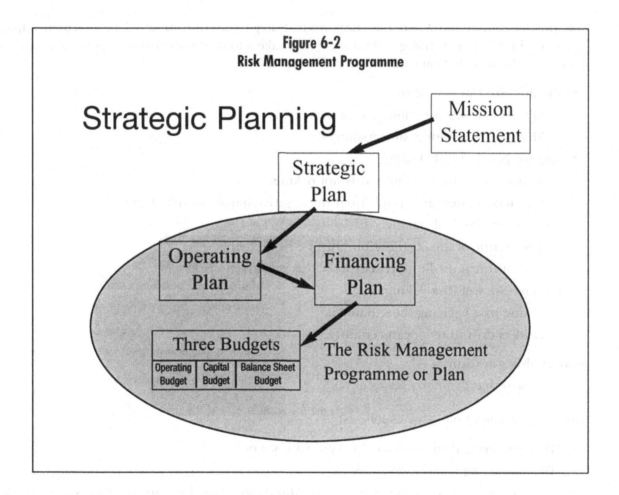

Your global risk management programme consists of your operating plan, financing plan, and the three budgets. *What goes terribly wrong in most organisations today is that the leaders see risk management as a function of insurance.* This job is assigned to the senior management accountant or a risk manager, a position that today many firms have outsourced or eliminated. The risk manager is rarely included in the strategic planning process. What this means is that your executives embark on a global plan, ignoring the risk or underestimating the risks' cost, and then turn the risk analysis over to the senior management accountant or risk manager. They drop it in that person's lap and ask, "Do we have adequate insurance coverage for this particular risk?"

This is a fatal blunder.

As you can see from the "Strategic Planning Flowchart" (figure 6-1), such actions will not really protect the firm. The risk management programme needs to be a foundational agenda item of strategic planning, performed offsite when the leaders work out what the plans are for next year. This is also the time they define what risk is, as described in step 1.

Strong risk management requires a team approach. An effective risk management programme consists of a cross-functional team of people throughout the organisation who examine risk holistically.

Risk's Two Faces

Now that we understand where risk starts (your strategic plan) and that risk management planning goes hand in glove with strategic planning, let us take a look at some planning paradoxes to understand how the organisation can effectively face up to risk:

- Paradox No. 1 of Risk Taking
  - Mistakes are an inevitable part of learning.
  - Mistakes waste money and resources.
- Paradox No. 2 of Risk Taking
  - A business is not growing if it is not risking.
  - Business failures often result from the negative impact of risks taken.
- Paradox No. 3 of Risk Taking
  - The culture of the organisation must be risk tolerant.
  - The culture must be able to expose areas sensitive to risks.
- Paradox No. 4 of Risk Taking
  - Taking risks is facing the unknown.
  - Leaders exist to reduce uncertainty.

Answer this question:
What are these four paradoxes saying to you?

Answers I hear most often are as follows:

- "They are saying damned if we do, damned if we don't."
- "They are saying risk is inevitable."
- "They tell me that as management accountants, we must be concerned about both sides of risk."
- "These paradoxes basically say that risk is inevitable, but we can do things to plan for them."

In a nutshell, what these paradoxes, together, are saying is that we cannot know everything, so we must be able to handle whatever risk occurs, especially those that we cannot foresee.

Answer this question:
How do these four paradoxes particularly affect management accountants?

Accounting Sits in the Middle

We in accounting and finance, especially if you are in a leadership role, are the people in the middle. We are in the midst of a very delicate high wire act, and we must make sure that we manage this balance very carefully. We cannot afford to push the organisation too far on one side. If we focus solely on the controls and checks and balances or we are rigid about people crossing all the t's and dotting the i's, we foster a culture in which nobody is willing to take any risk. History is littered with businesses that failed to out-innovate their competitors or keep up with the evolving marketplace.

On the other side of the balancing act, we have employees and leaders who want to be innovative, who strive to be creative, and who push the envelope on innovation, ideas, and processes. Our job is to support them—not let them undermine the success of the organisation. Why? For every company that has gone out of business because it failed to be innovative, there is a company that is history because it did not manage the risks it took.

The Cultural Aspect of Risk Taking and Risk Management

Write out how you would define workplace culture.

To me, workplace culture is ...

Your definition of culture is likely similar to others' because culture is instinctual in all of us. Any time two or three people join to work together on something, they create a culture. It is something that we humans do naturally.

Workplace culture is the mood, attitude, and atmosphere of an organisation. It is the story of who we are, as enacted by each employee. A shorthand for describing culture is: "How things are done around here."

What you may not know about culture (even though you have a good intuitive sense of what it is) is that culture is made up of 10 unique pieces. These 10 pieces fit together like a mosaic, and each one affects the other (see figure 6-3). They all must be in place for the mosaic to exist, and they must create a cohesive picture or image to be useful.

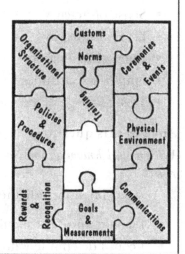

Figure 6-3
Culture Mosaic

The Cultural Mosaic Components:

- Communications
- Customs and Norms
- Physical Environment
- Rules and Policies
- Training
- Ceremonies and Events
- Goals and Measurement Process
- Leader's Attitudes, Behaviours, Beliefs
- Organisational Structure
- Rewards and Recognition

Your Culture Mosaic

Figure 6-4 is an image of how the mosaic pieces meld together. The centrepiece of all culture mosaics is the leader's attitudes, behaviours, and beliefs. This leader can be one person, a team, or a family.

When individuals decide to form an organisation or start a business, they gather other people around them who have like minds. We all have heard this description of some small businesses: "We are like a family." This describes a firm that consists of like-minded people sharing the same values and visions. All businesses start out this way, even Tesco, Standard Chartered Group, and Hyundai Motor.

Then, as the organisation grows and matures, the leader, realising the need for additional help, installs channels of communication. The firm grows into different physical locations, each with its own environment. The leader must set rules and policies to shape other people's behaviours. The organisation sets goals and creates tools to measure those goals. Because we want to reward people and maybe share the profits, we establish awards and recognition programs. We create an organisational structure because people must fill specific slots, wear fewer hats, or take on certain roles. Of course to promote fun, the leaders sponsor a holiday party or monthly birthday celebrations. Sometimes on their own or with guidance, employees start forming their own customs and norms. However, notice that the centre of the culture is still the leader's attitudes, behaviours, and beliefs. This centrepiece drives the entire culture from the beginning.

As the company grows older and the leader decides to hire professional managers because current leaders cannot do everything themselves or perhaps have grown incompetent, new leaders arrive and begin putting their imprint on the culture with new attitudes, behaviours, and beliefs. Even if this occurs, it takes years for the attitude, behaviour, and belief of the original founder to be fully removed.

By now you may be thinking, "Well this is great, but I am not my organisation's CEO. I am only a small cog in the machine, so what can I do about our culture?" I am glad you asked that question because that is where we are going next.

Visible Clues About Risk in Your Culture's Norms

There are some visible outcomes in your culture that will tell you what the organisation is like and what the culture says about its ability to handle risk. The areas that you need to keep your eye on and, if you are an auditor, need to examine carefully, include the following:

- Morale
- Sense of urgency
- Level of integrity
- Internal reputation
- Employees' attitudes
- Trust

- Behaviours involving ethics
- Loyalty
- Level of fun
- Cooperation
- Turnover rates
- Openness to the truth

Answer this question:

Why would knowing how your culture is built help you analyse your firm's ability to handle business risks?

Answers often include the following:

- "I would know if I should be concerned."
- "I could determine who most likely would follow through, and who wouldn't."

- "I could change the reward system to reward more risk taking."
- "We could evaluate the risky goals and get better feedback to determine if we're on track or should worry."
- "I believe that if employees are behind us [leaders], then we will more likely be successful, but if employees are against us, then our risk becomes greater."

That leads us to three more truisms of risk taking.

Risk management principles 4–6:

- Assessing and monitoring your culture will give you information about where you are vulnerable.
- Assessing and monitoring your culture will give you information on how your organisation values risk taking.
- Most organisations do not perform any formal risk analysis.

Morale Is Vital in Risk Awareness

You must always stay aware of employee morale and look to see if and when it changes. If it changes above or below the norm, you need to ask why. Maybe the morale has gone up temporarily because there is a surge in new sales orders. Or maybe morale has gone down and unbeknownst to you most of your employees are going to exit en masse. Recently a consultant in the human resources field cited several surveys that found over 80% of employees are unhappy at work because they do not like their jobs or employer, and they are actively looking for something else. Similarly 82% of executives are currently looking for new jobs.

Assume you are the CFO of an organisation undertaking a strategic initiative that generates a major risk. If you are successful, it will grow the company, but if not successful it will bankrupt the company. Would you (as CFO) want to know that 82% of your executive team is about to leave? Would that change your level of concern about the risk? Would you change how you look at the cost side of the risk?

Understanding your culture is important to proper risk management. Another reason why it is important is that you want to be capable of changing employees' attitudes toward taking more or less risks.

Culture Must Never Be Downplayed

In essence, culture is important because your culture brings forth success and failure with equal efficiency.

Culture is important, because the culture needs to expose risks rather than hide them. In many organisations, the norm is to hide risk, because the leaders always shoot the messenger. Rather than hear bad news, the leaders want people to dwell on the good news. In addition, they never want anyone to question or critique the strategies they conceive. So the prevailing culture becomes one in which employees will do anything to save their jobs, which includes sweeping unnecessary risks and problems under the rug.

Case Study

Analysis of Culture and Risk

From a gourmet food store chain (Gourmet) comes a tale of what happens if risks are not analysed in advance. Before Gourmet came out with its own line of rare spices, it entered into a joint venture with another organisation to create spice products to be sold through retail grocers. In this venture, Gourmet would provide the brand name and the partner would make the product. It launched the product, and soon thereafter, Gourmet's accounting team was asked to crunch the contract's numbers. A management accountant discovered that for every pint of ice cream sold under the Gourmet name Gourmet lost $1.75. Gourmet had locked themselves into a two-year contract with this organisation and could not modify the terms.

This story reminds us that everybody who will be affected by a risk must be involved in the discussion about the cost or potential impact. Accounting is very often not invited to the table when risks are explored—perhaps because the leaders know that we have the ability to look beyond the hype or upside potential of the risk. Yet, this critiquing is crucial to a reliable risk management programme.

Risk Analysis Tools

In a recent survey of CFOs and controllers, when asked if they use tools to quantify risk, they confessed that only one in 10 use any tools like these. *What does that say about the future of those nine out of 10 risk management programmes?*

Tools of Risk Identification

This is a two-part tool using questions and a flow chart that will help you, as a leader, to look at risk differently.

Part one of the tool is 5½ very important questions that need to be asked before a risk is undertaken. (figure 6-4)

Part two of this tool is known as *the critical risk path* (figure 5-6). Walking through this, step-by-step, before the organisation takes a major risk will help leaders and others to make smarter decisions.

Figure 6-4
Part One—Critical Risk Questions

What is the worst that can happen?

What is the best that can happen?

What is the most likely outcome?

What are the negative effects of the likely outcome?

How can we handle the negative effects?

How will we minimise or protect ourselves against the negative effects?

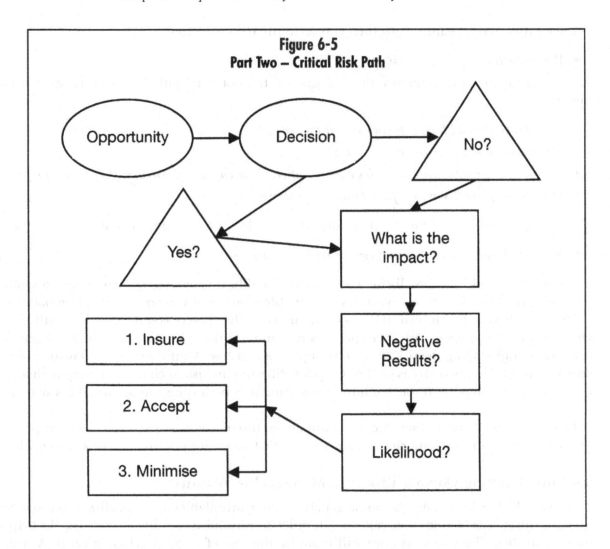

Figure 6-5
Part Two – Critical Risk Path

Let us see how they work together. Your firm sees an opportunity, for example, to do business in Russia. It is risky because you do not have any experience doing business there, and you hear stories about the crime and corruption that currently exist in Russia.

The upside of this opportunity is that a clear demand exists for your product with almost no competition. If you do not act swiftly, someone else could beat you there.

The question is: Do you open a sales branch in Russia? Do not assume that this tool is simplistic, because its value lies in what comes after your initial decision.

So you say "yes," we are going to open a branch in Russia.

Let us go to:

- *What is the impact?*
- *How will your business model change?*
- *How will you get the product there?*
- *How will you handle returns?*
- *What commission structure will work there?*
- *Will this affect your current customer base and, if so, how?*

You have identified the impact, so then you go to the next question.

- *What are the negative results?*

This is a great time to commence the dialogue on the potential pitfalls of the things that could hurt you.

- *How do we deal with corruption issues if they arise?*
- *How do we protect our employees' safety?*
- *Because we are using contract sales representatives, how can we ensure that they know the product?*
- *How do we prevent someone from pirating our design?*

The next question is very important because you now have to quantify the risk.

- *What is the likelihood of these negative results occurring?*

Quantify your risk by first listing each of the possible negative consequences and assigning a numerical likelihood. With experience, you will able to arrive at your own scale of probability.

Once you have a determined likelihood, you move to the choices you have to deal with the risk. One option is to accept it. Another option is to minimise the risk. There are plenty of actions to take before undertaking the risk to keep its impact or cost low. A third option is to insure, but that does not mean that insurance is your only option. Sharing the risk, such as partnering with another firm or putting a stop-loss through a limited investment of both time and money, is a way to insure the risk.

Best of all, your three options are not mutually exclusive. For example, you could accept part of the risk, insure part of it, and closely manage it so that you minimise the potential downsides.

Tool for Breaking Down a Risk Into Manageable Actions

This tool, which is known as a givens, negotiables, and controllables analysis, allows you to identify some of the specific actions you can take in order to minimise or mitigate the risk. To help you understand how the tool works, we will examine the risk of using purchasing cards. A number of companies are using purchasing cards, and every CFO or controller has warned others that you must go into this with your eyes wide open. It is not a simple solution, nor is it easy to implement. Most importantly, you must change or address certain things within your organisation and your culture in order to successfully use purchasing cards.

Steps

1. Write out a clear description of the risk to be undertaken:

   Soon we will begin using and issuing purchasing cards for every manager and supervisor. Most managers and supervisors are not trained adequately to deal with value-added tax and account code issues. No extra resources will be available to handle the additional administration of purchasing cards.

2. Prepare a chart that describes the various aspects:

Givens Aspects of the risk that we cannot control	Negotiables Aspects of the risk that we can influence or minimise	Controllables Aspects of the risk that we can use to address the danger
We must use purchasing cards for all supplies and related buys under $5,000.		
We do not know if our existing vendors will accept purchasing cards.		
We must be able to handle the administration of purchasing cards within existing A/P structure and staffing.		
The purchasing employee, who supported A/P, is no longer a resource for us.		
All managers will be issued a P card for use by their department.		

In this example, you will see that there are certain things that we have to accept, known as the *givens*. Second, there are parts of the risk that we can use to influence or minimise. These are known as the *negotiables*. Third, there are aspects of the risk that we can use to reduce the danger, and these are the *controllables*.

Exercise: What Would You Need?

In the space provided in figure 6-3, list some of the actions, either negotiable or controllable in nature, that you would want in place to minimise the risk of using purchasing cards.

Exercise: Givens, Negotiables, and Controllables

Use the following chart to analyse your firm's recent innovation, by breaking down a specific risk and defining its givens. Then, decide upon both things that you would ask for or put into place to protect the firm. Do not be too concerned whether your suggestions fall into the negotiable or controllable column.

Write out a clear description of the risk to be undertaken:

Givens Aspects of the risk that we cannot control.	Negotiables Aspects of the risk that we can influence or minimise.	Controllables Aspects of the risk that we can use to address the danger

Answer this question:

What did you discover or learn about being able to minimise risks using this particular tool?

In Essence

In step 3, you analyse the firm's ability to risk. It is very important for you as a leader and emerging risk manager to look at your firm's culture. Let us end this section with a peek at what a culture that balances risk taking and risk exposure looks like.

A Culture That Balances Risk Taking and Risk Exposure

What would an environment that balances risk taking and controls unnecessary risks look like?

> In the space provided, describe the qualities of a culture that balance risk taking exposure:

Answer these questions:

Does your organisation resemble any of these?

Which ones do you lack? Check them off.

The most common responses are as follows:

- "Good communication"
- "People leading by example"
- "Tools for employees to use"
- "A team approach to risk management"
- "A culture of positive reports"
- "A culture where we do not shoot the messenger"
- "A balanced approach to risk taking"
- "A concern that every risk has a cost"
- "An awareness about what a risk is and what it could look like"
- "Sensitivity to risk"
- "Accountability"
- "A culture where employees are encouraged to raise their concerns and issues"

- "A culture of sharing"
- "Leaders who are more concerned about the company's success than their own success"
- "Transparency"

The Point

The lesson in taking time to identify the ideal culture that balances risk taking and risk exposure is that as a leader you must assess your company's culture and the firm's ability to afford the risks that you choose to undertake.

Here are several suggestions on what your culture should look like.

How to Generate a Balanced Risk Taking Culture

1. *Create the environment*—A risk taker-friendly environment is one in which people are invited to take reasonable challenges.

2. *Forget the procedures*—Goals and outcomes always count more than strict adherence to procedures.

3. *Instil flexibility*—A flexible approach to problems permits innovation.

4. *Encourage people*—Leaders create an environment in which good people are nurtured, supported, and encouraged to build upon their strengths.

5. *Trust people*—Demonstrate that you trust them regardless of the outcome.

6. *Foster change*—A risk-friendly environment sees change as good and desirable.

7. *Be reliable*—People will risk when they feel safe and can rely on the leader. The leader models the behaviour you want others to have.

8. *Control the odds*—Set limits on the losses, never risking more than you can afford.

9. *Know your people*—Leaders must understand their own risk-taking attitude and those of the people around them.

10. *Know your limits*—There will always be things that you want to do and cannot and things that you are not doing that you can, so you need to know the subtle difference.

10½. *You go first*—Leaders must take more personal risks than their followers.

Culture's Impact on Risk Taking

Paradox of business success:

- Enjoy and capitalise on the good times.
- In the good times, you must look for impending dangers.

In the good times, it is easy to forget about risk. Yet it is during the upswings that executives need to be most watchful for the signs of impending danger. In aggressive "can do" or "grow at all cost" forms of cultures, when bold initiatives are being set and customers are coming in the door, it is usual to silence the messenger who carries bad news about the company's strategy or practices.

Success should make leaders nervous. As we know, not every risk is bad, and in order to survive today, we must take risks in order to make progress. Yet leaders are less aware of risk exposure than those closer to the operations. Likewise, employees closer to the operations are aware of the risks that affect their area but are blind to or underestimate the impact on other parts of our organisation. Therefore, understanding the conditions that create unnecessary levels of risk allows us to help prevent failure, while taking advantage of opportunities.

A business cannot survive over the long-term or prosper without entrepreneurial risk taking that leads to innovation and creativity. However, success can give some risk takers, especially CEOs, too much confidence to the point at which they harm the company's assets and reputation, all in the pursuit of greater gains. (Read "The Mind-Set of the Risk Taking Entrepreneur" in chapter 5, "Step Two—Examine Attitudes Toward Risk.") This may be a virtually irresistible urge in organisations with meteoric success. Often, in a successful firm that has never experienced a loss, people move toward excessively risky deals, forge alliances with others who do not have the ability to honour their contracts, or make promises to customers that are impossible to fulfil. The catalyst for this type of behaviour is the rewards built into the cultural norms. These rewards are both overt and hidden. As the rewards for entrepreneurial behaviour grow, so does risk exposure. Therefore, leaders must also reward clever decision making through risk evaluation and assessment.

There are two relationships regarding risk in a culture. The first is the one we all know, the ratio of risk and reward. The second one of equal importance is the relationship between risk and awareness. What sinks a company is not necessarily the risks themselves but the ignorance about the potential consequences of each viable risk. If managers are aware of the risks—their source, nature, and magnitude—they can take appropriate steps to avoid or mitigate the hidden pitfalls. This ability is critical in the operational areas or front lines of an organisation. The more our people know where risk resides in our organisation, the more quickly they can respond and react.

Risk Inherent in Your Culture

Intentionally or unintentionally, organisations may teach employees to cheat or embezzle based upon their policies. These policies can drive employee behaviour in ways that we never expected.

Your employees' tendency to take advantage of you through unwarranted risk or fraud can be described on a normal distribution curve.

- 5% to 10% of your employees will never do anything unethical or be rash.
- 5% to 10% of your employees are always looking for ways to take advantage of you.
- 80% to 90% of your employees will commit situational fraud or take unwarranted risk when it is to their advantage.

Walk in My Shoes

I work hard putting in innumerable hours, including weekends, to meet an impossible deadline. I complete the project for you on time. I ask you for a couple of days off to recuperate and replace the time I could not spend with my family. You point out to me the firm's policy says, "Employees can only take time off for sick leave or holiday." If you were in my shoes, what would you do? Get mad? Accept it? Get back to work?

Guess what I (and most of your employees) will do? I will either take time off telling you I am sick (even though I am not), or I will come to the office but not really work for a few days.

You probably feel that I should be fired for this unprofessional behaviour. But because you have chosen, as my supervisor, to stay rigid on the policy and not give me any consideration for the extra effort I put into your project, you placed me into a situation in which I chose to default to my own ethical values.

Unfortunately, we cannot expect ethical behaviour from our employees unless we executives and leaders model ethical behaviour first. You must walk the walk and talk the talk in fairness, equity, and ethics every day. Unless you live up to the highest level of integrity, you will not be able to demand this of anyone else in your organisation.

Summary: Importance of Step 3

A risk management programme is more an attitude than a written document. The heart of the attitude is the firm's corporate culture. However a culture is often neglected, ignored, or overlooked by leaders of business organisations. That is why we spend so much time understanding what a culture is and how it affects risk. Risk starts with the firm's strategies, which are the tools that the firm's leaders develop to carry out a business model.

In step 3 of your risk management plan, you must spend time understanding the components of the cultural mosaic and the risk inherent in those strategies, and then use this information to identify specific risks. Once you have identified the risks, you apply the tools in this section to determine the level of their impact. After you have identified this, then the firm quantifies the amount of money that needs to be dedicated from your three budgets to help mitigate or cover the cost of those risks.

This step is ongoing and is never completed because of the nature of the firm's global strategies—they are always changing and evolving. This aspect of the firm's risk management plan changes and evolves as well.

7

Step Four—Minimise the Risk Exposure

Small issues swell into huge problems when ignored.

After reading this chapter, you should be able to

- apply three specific tools to help strategise and minimise the negative impact of a major risk.
- develop some specific ways that people in your organisation can be proactive in minimising the negative effects of risk.
- understand why risk taking requires employees to think for themselves.
- begin to delve into the real cause of a major risk.

Because avoidance of risk is not possible, it is better to be proactive in minimising any negative or costly consequences of innovation, creativity, and colouring outside the lines.

This chapter, step 4, gives you the tools to do that. If every employee within your organisation knew how to use these tools to mitigate the risk of success, you would have a healthy company with a viable future.

Risk Mitigation Tools

At the beginning of this book, you were asked to think of a particular risk that your organisation is undertaking. You now can define the optimal strategy to use based on where your exposure falls in the matrix shown as figure 7-1. This tool helps you to quantify risk based on two variables—likelihood and negative impact.

Exercise: Risk Strategy Grid

Instructions

Recall the risk your organisation is undertaking. Define your strategy based on where your exposure falls into the grid in figure 7-1.

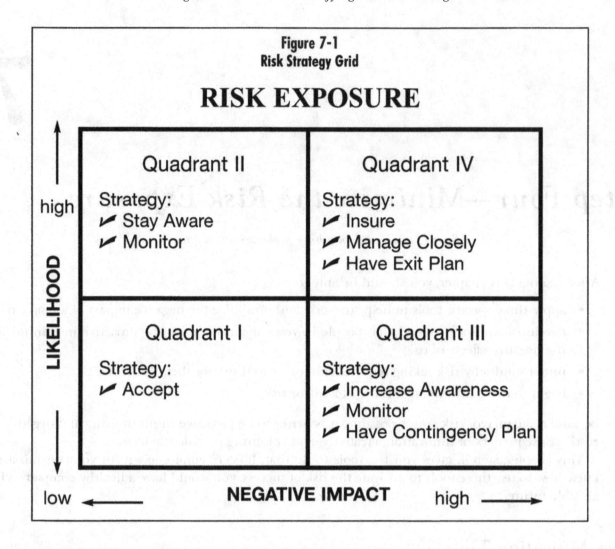

This risk strategy grid is a common matrix that is often used to assist decision makers to foster smarter decisions. It applies to effective risk management as well.

Let us refer to the risk exposure of opening a sales office in Russia from chapter 6, "Step Three— Analyse the Firm's Ability to Handle Risk." Your main concern is the finances of your firm, because opening the sales office will tie up a big chunk of capital and you need an immediate 30% return on investment (ROI) to counter that risk. After careful analysis of the decisions and their impact, long-and short-term, you decide that the negative impact on your finances is low and the likelihood of this new operation turning sour is very low. This places your risk in quadrant I, and your optimal strategy is accepting, meaning that your leaders recognise that some problems could exist, but they are committed to not letting them stop their plans.

Alternatively, if this risk means that the negative impact on your financial situation is low and the likelihood of not obtaining the immediate 30% return is high, your strategy will be in quadrant II of staying aware and monitoring.

Possible solutions are that you institute an incentive for the store's manager that fosters day-by-day awareness of some of the things that could occur or go wrong. At your organisation's headquarters, you designate specific people assigned to look at the selected metrics daily to ensure that everything is going according to plan.

If opening this store in Russia is one in which the likelihood of not obtaining the immediate 30% ROI is low, but the risk of negative drain on your cash position is high, then you would adopt a strategy in quadrant III of *increasing awareness, monitoring,* and most importantly *having a contingency plan.* The awareness and monitoring are the same as in quadrant II, but it is at a higher tension level. You make sure everyone knows that if this venture is not managed properly, the entire company can be in trouble. Your contingency plan is to create a reserve fund, or to prequalify a Russian partner that you could offer partial ownership to, or to send your best manager to run the Russian store.

Finally, the most costly risk is the one that falls into quadrant IV. This venture, if it turns worse than anticipated, has both a high negative impact and a high likelihood of failure. Because we elected to take the risk, we adopt specific strategies equal to the level of risk. Those strategies include *insuring, managing closely,* and most importantly, *deciding on an exit plan.*

Failure to have an exit plan can come back to harm you. Some organisations continue to dig themselves into a deeper hole because the leaders refuse to believe that failure is a possibility. The belief that "failure is not an option" worked fine for Apollo 13, but I know very few shareholders who support executives that throw good money at bad opportunities. There were a lot of dotcoms that became dotbombs, whose only business model was to set up a company, then have an initial public offering so they could cash out as millionaires. When their business model proved to be worthless, they did not have any alternatives lined up.

Answer this question:

How can this tool help to reduce the negative effects of undertaking your significant risk?

That leads us to risk management principles 7–8:

- The negative impact of risk taking is greatly reduced when you analyse the real cause of the undesirable results.

- Because you cannot control all risks, it is much healthier to be prepared for the worst and expect the best.

Proactive Attitudes

Let us explore some specific ways that you can be proactive in minimising the negative effects of risk.
What are practical ways to be proactive toward exposure to the negative impact of risk taking?
Compare your answers with the list that follows:

Ways to be Proactive in Minimising Negative Effects of Risks

☐ *Check your ego at the door.* Leaders with a strong belief in themselves and their ideas can easily impose their will on others.

☐ *Keep asking, "But what about...?"* In today's changing environment, there is a fine line between being decisive and being blind.

☐ *Nobody is as clever as everybody.* Many leaders fail to involve others in their strategic decisions. If you want visionaries, you must first build visionaries.

☐ *Simple mistakes do not have simple causes.* Simple mistakes often involve more than one person, which means you are facing group dynamics or cultural problems.

☐ *Little mistakes yield big insights.* If we act a certain way with the small things, we will act the same way with the big things.

☐ *What gets measured gets monitored.* What gets rewarded gets repeated. What are you measuring and why? What are you rewarding and why?

☐ *Wake up.* Leaders must influence people to consciousness about risk's reality.

☐ *Assess your risks.* Set a valid basis for your decisions.

☐ *Inspire people with your internal control system.* Controls must not be made to prevent action, but to allow people to take it.

☐ *Information is the "Breakfast of Champions."* Help people to know what information is needed and why.

Check off all those that you are currently practising. (Be honest.)

Importance of Step 4

The essence of step 4 is to minimise your firm's risk exposure, or better yet to inspire actions to lower the cost of failure. The next part of your risk action plan is to perform an authority and responsibility analysis.

An underlying purpose of an effective risk management programme is to foster constant awareness of everyone throughout your organisation about risks—large and small. Leaders, all too often, make a mistake that is detrimental to fostering awareness. As managers and supervisors, we give employees the responsibility for something, yet fail to give them the authority to take action. In proper risk management, when we ask people to be accountable and empowered about doing things to reduce risk or cost, we must be 100% sure that we have given the specific authority equal to that responsibility.

Disempowerment Inaction

This happened to me recently:

I am leaving the next morning for an out-to-town consulting project. I stop at a large office supply store chain to get some hard-to-find protective covers that I use for documentation purposes. I find only one box of 50, but it has been opened. I search around but cannot find other boxes. I take my purchase to the counter and show the clerk the torn box and ask her if she can locate another box. She checks and says, "No, that is our last box." I express my concern that there could be some protectors missing so she counts and finds only 49 sheets. At that point the sales clerk does not know what to do next.

I am anxious to get going because I have several things to do before I call it a day. She is the only cashier and now several customers wait impatiently behind me. Because the clerk is at a loss she calls for a manager. We wait and we wait. I suggest, "Just deduct 5 cents from the box price to cover the cost of the missing protector." She replies, "I'm not authorised to give any discounts." We wait and we wait. That evening, the office supply store chain created much ill will, not because of 5 cents, but because their culture is one in which employees are not empowered to act.

Employees Who Think for Themselves

Compare the example with the Marriott Hotel group. Marriott has a policy for all its frontline employees: "You can spend up to $2,000 to satisfy any customer problem." There are five questions that Marriott employees must answer to themselves before they give or spend money to solve the problem. The five questions posed to employees are as follows:

1. Will this action harm the reputation of the hotel? ____
2. Will this action cause a problem for another guest? ____
3. Will this action only defer a problem? ____
4. Will this action upset the guest even more? ____
5. Is this action illegal or unethical? ____

If the answer to all five questions are "no," the employees can take the action they deem necessary to satisfy a guest or a customer.

What Marriott has learned from their empowering policy is that it usually takes somewhere around $100 to satisfy the customer or solve the problem. It might be buying the guest a meal, picking up his or her cab fare, comping one night's stay at another hotel, or providing a gift such as a bottle of champagne or wine. Rarely, if ever, is the entire $2,000 spent.

Answer this question:

Do you trust in your employees enough that you would give each of them $2,000 of company's cash and trust them to use it only to save a client relationship without going to someone for approval?

Fewer than 25% would feel comfortable doing this. If you are among the 75% who feel uncomfortable, then your firm, like many organisations, may be unable to equate responsibility with authority. This type of culture will undermine an effective risk management programme.

Balanced Risk Taking Requires Employees Thinking for Themselves

During a class I taught, a wise woman summarised the importance of this need to equate authority with responsibility. She did not give her name, so I cannot give her credit for this astute observation. She told the class:

"If you make employees responsible for unlocking the door, give them the key."

In your organisation, you are asking employees to monitor for risk—asking them to unlock the door—but you are not giving them the tools, the knowledge, or the authority to do something about the risk. You and other leaders refuse to give employees the key to the door.

A risk management programme requires employees at every level, who are making decisions and taking action, to let leaders know when there is something going wrong. Employees need to believe and know that they will not be punished for blowing the whistle or waving the red flag. Leaders need to strive to match authority with responsibility so that employees can and will think for themselves.

In figure 7-2, you will see the two circles coming together. Your goal is to try to match them up as closely as possible. You will never get it to be a 100% match, because the need for internal control affects empowerment and authority. These checks and balances need to be seen as empowering employees to take action and not as impediments.

Figure 7-2
Matching Responsibility with Authority

PEOPLE WHO THINK FOR
THEMSELVES

Authority = Responsibility

Your Goal!

PEOPLE WHO THINK FOR
THEMSELVES

Authority = Responsibility

Your Goal!

Tool to Perform an Authority and Responsibility Analysis

Answer these questions:

Where have you defined each decision maker's authority to represent the company?

How is it communicated?

How is it updated to reflect change?

Does the average employee know of its existence or even its contents?

Do you use any type of authority or responsibility chart? How does it work?

A tool that will allow you to equate responsibility with authority is called a risk authority and responsibility chart (figure 7-3). You will notice in this tool that you can easily highlight specific areas of concern, in this case, internal control over actions and decisions.

Figure 7-3
Risk Authority and Responsibility Tool

Authority and Responsibility Chart	Accounting Manager	Credit Manager	Controller	VP of Finance
Set policy	R	R	R	A
Finalise procedures	A	A	I	I
Hire from outside	R	R	R	R
Hire from inside	R	R	R	A
Institute compensation programmes	R	No	R	A
Make purchases and expenses:				
Ordinary supplies	$100	$300	$5,000	$50,000
Expense reports	$100	$100	$1,000	$2,500
Travel plans	No	No	A	A
Capital equipment	R	R	R	A
Credit memos:	R	A	R	R
Adjustment to inventory	R	R	A	R
Write-off inventory	R	No	R	A
Price adjustments	R	No	No	R
Adjust customer Accounts Receivable	$100	$25,000	$50,000	No
Issue special customer terms	I	A	I	I
Public relations:				
Speak for company	No	No	No	R
Issue press releases	No	R	R	R
Security:				
Alarm system access	Yes	Yes	Yes	Yes
Computer system access	Yes	Yes	Yes	Yes
Warehouse access	Tour Only	No	Yes	Yes

Legend

$ Dollar amounts show maximum approval limits per event
R   Recommend
A   Approve
I   Be informed

Figure 7-3 shows three symbols signifying authority and responsibility: the *R* means that the person could recommend the action; the *A* means that the person has the authority for the action; and *I* means the person is to be informed. Remember, even though it is your job to keep me informed, it is my job to stay informed—communication is a dual responsibility.

Notice that the accounting manager, credit manager, and controller can recommend a policy, but final approval and authority rests with the vice president of finance. This makes sense because the vice president has a concern for the big picture. When adopting procedures, the actual people doing the work (the credit and accounting managers) have the authority to make it happen. Their responsibility also includes keeping the vice president and controller informed.

Look at the structure for the issuance of credit memos halfway down on the chart. This hypothetical organisation has a problem with inventory adjustments. Every year for the prior five, the book inventory has had to be adjusted downward, and nobody has been able to find the source of the discrepancy. Ultimately, the controller found that anyone and everyone could make general ledger (GL) adjustments to our book inventory. The controller's first action was to clamp down and stop these entries. She used this tool to create restrictions on who could make adjustments to our GL inventory. Notice that the accounting manager and credit manager could recommend inventory adjustment entries, but they required her approval. Even the vice president could not adjust our inventory. Before she changed this system, both the credit and accounting managers could adjust inventory without restriction. With this control in place, now she would know.

For the decision to write off inventory, the accounting manager could have reasons to recommend the write-off, but the controller could not see any reason why the credit manager would need to. In fact, she felt that would be a conflict of interest for him to the make inventory cost or valuation adjustments.

Similarly, when it came to adjusting specific customer accounts, the controller limited the accounting manager's authority to $100, which would cover minor things like deductions or charge backs. Her credit manager could adjust a customer account up to $25,000, and if the issue was larger, he would come to her. If, in the rare instance the inventory adjustment entry was more than $50,000, they needed the CEO's approval. Notice that even the vice could not adjust customer accounts.

Five Why's Tool

This is a tool used by many organisations in some form or another. One way to make it tool even more effective is to house it on the company intranet. Then, if employees or managers want to understand what control procedures are involved in an action or decision, they click on the hyperlink and go to the Web page that provides that information. Additionally, let us say that you decide to increase your accounting manager's purchase authority for office supplies from $100 to $1,000. You can do that quickly online. This tool gives you flexibility, while defining and communicating authority and responsibility and developing control awareness over risks.

Answer these questions:

How would this tool help your organisation decrease the negative impact of risks that you undertook?

How would this tool decrease the negative impact of risks?

How would this tool increase accountability in risk taking?

Tool to Analyse the Causes of Exposure

This tool, known as the *Five Why's*, allows us to find the root causes of risks that can lead to detrimental effects. The cause of the downside of risk taking is rarely from physical things such as plants or hardware. Most of the time, they are generated or caused by how people think and act.

In this example, an empowered product manager purchased products that he felt the company could sell. Because the company emphasised to all of its purchasing employees that they needed to use their best judgement when dealing with the vendors and making purchasing decisions on their product line, they almost always had the final say. The company thought it had in place clearly defined policies. It found out that this was a false assumption. The product manager contracted the company for a product that later did not sell and was later discovered not to be returnable.

The Five Why's has four simple steps, but do not be fooled by its simplicity. It is the questions that you keep asking *after* you get your initial answers that makes it so powerful. As management accountants, our task is to find the root cause of a problem. We often waste so much time finding and removing the smoke that we never get to the cause of the fire. This tool allows us to discover what caused the fire so that we can prevent the fire from starting again.

Steps of Five Why's:

1. State the risk as a problem.

2. Ask: "Why is this happening?"

3. Continue to ask why until you get to a root cause that (*a*) you can do something about, and (*b*) when reduced or eliminated, the situation will change for the better.

4. Summarise your findings.

Example of a Risk Exposure
Using the decision-making tool called Five Why's, let us try to find the root causes of a common and specific exposure to a risk.

Statement of Problem

Empowered product manager obliges our company for a product that does not sell and is nonreturnable.

Now that we know the problem, we ask the first question:

1. Why did this happen?
   The manager did not adhere to the company's policy for acquiring a new product line.

We discover through investigation that the manager did not adhere to the company's policy for acquiring a new product. Our policy in part states, "A product manager may not agree to purchase a product or product derivation that is designated by the supplier as nonreturnable... Any exceptions must be approved in advance by the vice president of operations."

Typically, most of us would stop at the first why and would fire that product manager for violating a policy. If we do that, however, all we have accomplished is to deal with the smoke and failed to search for the cause of the fire. So by being good, astute, and smart people, we want to prevent the fire. We ask again:

2. Why did this happen?
   The manager wants to impress the vendor.

Maybe it was a new relationship or something similar. But we find that this product manager agreed to this contract based on the personality of the vendor.

We proceed to ask again:

3. Why did this happen?
   The manager is looking for something above the ordinary.

We find several instances in our research that this manager has done this before—seeking out special conditions in his initial dealings with other new vendors.

Let us review ethical implications. As a management accountant who is concerned with the ethical attitude of this person, you might jump up and down and demand this employee be fired. But you do not know if this situation is an isolated event or might be happening with other employees.

Back to the tool, you ask again:

4. Why did this happen?

The manager wants to get paid his large incentive bonus.

You uncover that the manager wanted to get paid his large semi-annual incentive bonus.

Now we are starting to get to the root cause. By using this tool regularly, you will find the root cause is often based around power, emotion, drive, greed, or lust. Some human frailty is involved with lingering problems, especially those related to unwarranted risk taking and ethical breaches.

We ask again:

5. Why did this happen?

The incentive rewards employees for increasing the product line and does not penalise them for inventory that does not sell.

We discover that the incentive programme for all product managers was designed for them to expand the product line's diversity. The incentive contains no penalty or downside for inventory that does not sell. Whoever set up the incentive felt the need for people to bring inventory in the door, but failed to hold them responsible for the inventory once it was on the shelf.

Again, we could stop there, but your intuition tells you there could be another cause for the fire.

You do not have to stop at five why's; you can go on with as many as possible, but usually five or six is enough to get to the fire's cause.

6. Why did this happen?

The emphasis on managing inventory levels and turns is seen as a function (responsibility) of the inventory control group, which reports to the controller. The product managers report to the operations manager.

The responsibility and the controls over managing inventory levels and inventory turns are viewed as accounting's area of expertise. This key control function has been given to the inventory control manager, who reports to the controller. The product manager reports to the operations manager, a function completely outside accounting.

Answer these questions:

In this example, what do you see as the real risk?

Now that we know the cause, what can we do to affect it? In other words, what needs to be done to prevent the fire from happening again?

The Real Risk

What we discovered in using the Five Why's tool is that we split the authority with responsibility. We made the purchasing group accountable for the purchasing side of inventories and made accounting accountable for the control side of inventories. By not paying attention to which behaviours we reward, we split responsibility and authority.

The lesson from this tool is that when we find the root cause for the possible negative impact of risk taking, we can take more intelligent actions to reduce the negative effects.

Exercise: Finding the Root Cause

The following is a blank form listing the Five Why's for you to use. You are encouraged to think of specific risks or problems and go through the Five Why's and conduct interviews to discover why your problem or risk is a reality.

Instructions

Following the example on the previous page and using Five Why's, try to find the root cause of one of your firm's specific exposures to risk.

The Exposure:

1. Why could (did) this occur?

2. Why could (did) this occur?

3. Why could (did) this occur?

4. Why could (did) this occur?

5. Why could (did) this occur?

Conclusion:

What seems to be a possible root cause of your risk exposure?

Tool for Isolating the Optimal Solutions

A tool called a Criteria Checkerboard allows us to analyse the exposure of a specific risk and then use the information to determine how to proceed. It is a key tool used by consultants for defining and matching the criteria for success with the possible alternatives. Using this information, you can analyse your exposure to a risk and then use the data to decide the best solution or path to take.

Steps for the Criteria Checkerboard

1. Select your criteria for a best decision
2. Brainstorm alternative solutions
3. List the criteria and alternatives on a checkerboard
4. Check off how well each solution meets your criteria

Example of a Risk Exposure

Your information system is vulnerable to sabotage by outsiders.
 Which of your plans is the best solution to reduce the exposure?
 We will walk through the tool by using an example of our exposure.
 Our existing (and very old) information system is vulnerable to sabotage from outside the organisation. Your leaders made a risky decision to spend a pool of funds to generate sales using the Internet, leaving insufficient funds to upgrade your current technology. You, the controller, informed the

leadership team of your concerns. They instruct you to recommend the most viable and optimal solution within these three specific constraints:

1. The fix must make your system invulnerable.
2. The fix must not cost a lot.
3. The fix must be easy to implement without adding any people to the IT staff.

Because your leaders have increased your firm's exposure and therefore your risk, you need to find an optimal solution to lower the cost of vulnerability. You also need to find the best solution out of a series of options. (And show the leaders that their restrictions are unrealistic.)

The first step of the tool is to select specific criteria for the best decision. Then, brainstorm alternative solutions that could possibly work to solve the problem. Next, list our criteria and alternatives on the checkerboard. Finally, compare how well each solution or alternative fits into the criteria.

The key part is selecting the specific criteria. Your criterion decides what will make a good decision so that you minimise the risk's impact. This is always your starting point. Our leaders gave us three things they wanted:

- Make our system invulnerable
- Keep the cost for additional security low
- Find a solution that is easily implemented without adding staff

Next, once you have the criterion, and before you determine whether they are valid, you select some alternatives or potential courses of action. In selecting alternatives, you want to use the rules of good brainstorming. This means that every idea is acceptable and possible, and no ideas are too outrageous. Write down every idea as it is presented and remain open to the idea no matter what the source or the rationale for it.

Our solutions team brainstormed several ideas, including the following:

- Disconnect from the Internet
- Monitor the system 24 hours a day, 7 days a week.
- Outsource our entire IT function.
- Employ a high-end firewall.
- Require that employees change their passwords weekly.

Possible Alternatives	*Criteria 1:* *Makes system* *invulnerable*	*Criteria 2:* *Keeps cost for* *security low*	*Criteria 3:* *Is easily implemented* *without adding staff*
Disconnect from the Internet			
Monitor the system 24/7			
Outsource our IT function			
Employ a high-end firewall			
Change passwords weekly			

Later, you go back and narrow the list down to the more reasonable or realistic alternatives. In this example, we already narrowed down (through the rules of good brainstorming) four viable alternatives. Now your job is to go through the checklist and compare all the alternatives with your three criteria or restrictions.

You will notice that the only alternative that meets the restriction of "make our system invulnerable" is to disconnect from the Internet. Yet we need access to the Web to do business. Now you have proof that your firm's executives know nothing about technology. So we toss out that criterion.

You will notice that the restriction of "low cost" is too vague. This needs more definition.

You will also notice that alternatives "employ a high-end firewall" and "change passwords weekly" can be combined into one.

You know, of course, that outsourcing IT has severe repercussions and is not something you do just to avoid someone getting into your system. While it meets criterion 3 "no more IT staff," there is no guarantee that your IT service vendor's system will be any less vulnerable than yours.

After further work, your team arrives at an alternative that meets most of the executives' concerns.

"Implement a complete security plan that includes changing passwords monthly, increased monitoring, employing a high-end firewall, and training employees on security issues every month."

Now that we applied the tool, answer these questions:

- *How will this reduce our exposure to the negative consequences of having a vulnerable information system?*
- *Which of these alternatives meets our need for "Best Solution"?*
- *Why is it optimal?*
- *How would this reduce our exposure to the negative consequences of having a vulnerable information system?*

The lesson from this narrative is that because every risk has a cost, it is important to use decision-making tools to uncover these costs and possible negative downsides.

Summary: Importance of Step 4

Once we have convinced people in the organisation that we need to treat a specific risk seriously, step 4 starts us moving toward taking action and placing tools in the hands of employees so they can make smarter decisions. There is an old saying, "Fully warned is fully armed." Except for strategic risk or faulty assumptions in the business plan, it is rare that an executive identifies a particular operational risk. It is almost always an employee who is doing the work and dealing with the situation who recognises a cost we cannot afford. Our job as leaders is to help the employees at this level define the seriousness of the problem, so they can take action.

8

Step Five—Recover From the Negative Results

Risk Happens!

After reading this chapter, you should

- understand how a contingency plan works.
- be able to prepare a pitfall analysis.
- be able to develop a lessons learned programme for your team or company.
- recognise and explain the importance of the risk management audit.

Despite our best planning, anticipating, and analysis, there will always be things that we cannot anticipate, or our implementation goes awry, or we make human errors in judgement. Yes, even leaders can be wrong.

An imperative in your risk management plan is created when employees within your organisation have a specific methodology for recovering quickly from a negative result. The important element in this step is to make sure that you hone your recovery skills on the small lapses.

For example, say that you get the itch to run a marathon. You are not a runner and have never run one before. Instead of going out and immediately trying to run 42 kilometres, health experts will tell you that you prepare by taking small steps. Your first task is walking and setting a milestone of being able to walk two hours without stopping. Next you alternate walking and jogging until you can go a kilometre without stopping. Your next task is to build up stamina until you can run that kilometre without walking. When you are comfortable with a kilometre, you extend it to two kilometres and then three. You continue with these smaller goals until you are able to run more than 42 kilometres in one outing. Can you do this in one day or even one month?

Of course not.

The same holds true for good risk management. We must use the same tools and methodology on smaller, less costly risks, so when a larger risk crops up, one that has a terrible cost of failure, we can face it with confidence. Soon, your firm will have the ability to recover quickly no matter what unexpected things occur. The more you use a muscle, the stronger it becomes. Similarly, the more you practise risk management in your day-to-day decisions, the stronger your programme becomes.

Here is a good example that likely hits close to home. Your firm probably has a backup mechanism for your information and data collection system. Has anyone in your firm thought to test a dry run of that system?

We assume that the backup system works because it collects and mirrors the original data. But we riskily assume that when the unthinkable occurs, this backup system will take us back to the point before the failure. The only way to know for sure is to actually crash your system several times and jump start with the backup system.

No one wants to tackle all that work of verifying each data point because of the time and effort it will take to do so. Why are you accepting this clearly identifiable risk?

Risk Recovery Tools

The more you practise risk management in your day-to-day decisions, the stronger your programme becomes.

Tool for Pitfall Planning

A tool for helping you to recover quickly is a pitfall analysis. This tool works not only for management accountants, but also for people who typically do not think long-term or analytically and critically. This tool forces them to think that way. Using this decision-making tool, we can create ways to learn lessons from exposure to a risk.

Steps of Pitfall Analysis

1. List the possible pitfalls of a particular course of action.
2. Create contingency action plans for each pitfall.
3. Determine what would prevent implementing the plan.

An example we will use to understand this tool is one that many management accountants have experienced and one fraught with exposure: converting to a new accounting software platform. Assume that this is a major upgrade. You have been using a middle-market type of software and decide to go big time and invest in a million dollar real-time database platform. For those of you who have gone through one of these conversions, you know that it is a minefield.

In this example, assume the following:

You, as a lead on this project, identify these potential and common pitfalls:

Pitfall	Contingency Plan
Losing a key member of the conversion team, especially Alberto or Isabel.	Hire qualified temporary for length of conversion project to support Isabel and Alberto
Conversion process takes longer than expected.	Spend more time planning up front and hold weekly update meetings with conversion team.
Cost of conversion is more than the budget established three years ago.	Prepare an updated cost projection with help of consultant.
	Request budget update meeting with CEO ASAP.

Answer this question:

How would this tool help you to minimise the negative effects of the exposure and recover more quickly?

Exercise: Risk Analysis

Instructions

In the space that follows, you have an opportunity to think of risk that you, your team, or your firm is facing and list the potential pitfalls and your recommended contingency plans. Do not forget that contingency plans also include allocating or budgeting money to spend for that particular problem. There is a prevailing belief in budgeting that using contingency funds is a bad thing. There are risks, but if they are handled correctly, you can turn them into a positive aspect and an asset to your risk management programme.

Describe Your Exposure:

Potential Pitfall	Suggested Contingency Plan
1.	
2.	
3.	
4.	
5.	
6.	
Is there anything that can prevent you from undertaking these plans?	

Contingency Funds in Risk Management

Let us go back to your exposure of opening a store in Russia in chapter 6, "Step Three—Analyse the Firm's Ability to Handle Risk." For the next year, as you expand your presence there and establish a beachhead, you include a contingency fund of $50,000 in your current year's budget. This $50,000 can only be spent under three conditions:

1. If the sales in Russia fail to reach $2,000,000

2. If the potential customers do not become aware of your product, based on an independent survey

3. If the method of advertising through the most popular newspapers proves ineffective in attracting consumer attention

Only if all three conditions are met can the $50,000 be used to hire sales agents to sell your product and offer cash-back incentives to storm your way into the marketplace. If during the year only one or two of those conditions are met, this fund cannot be used, even if sales continue to look bleak. And this contingency fund cannot be used for any other purposes, such as bailing out stores in your home country because the manager there is inept and you will not earn your incentive bonus because of him.

If these three conditions do not happen in the current year, then you carry the contingency fund over to next year. You can maintain or modify the conditions under which the money can be spent.

This is how to properly handle a contingency fund. After a certain point of time—say the Russian stores meet all sales, profit, and return on investment targets—the funds can then be returned by reversing the contingency expense, thus adding to the current year's profits because of good management.

When we take the time to look for pitfalls and then develop contingency plans in advance, we grow in confidence in our ability to face or accept more risk.

Tool for Fostering a Lessons Learned Attitude

Another way to help build up your muscles for recovering quickly is to adopt a lessons learned programme into your cultural norms. It needs to become a critical part of your culture mosaic. All organisations with effective risk management programmes use this technique, though they may refer to it in different terminology. Yet, consistently, firms that are proactive in quickly identifying and mitigating risk rely heavily on their lessons learned from risks taken.

Answer this question:

What kind of lessons learned process does your organisation have?

That leads us to the next truism.

Risk management principle 9:

- It is much easier to recover from negative impact of risk taking and unexpected challenges when you have taken the time to learn from previous challenges.

Your lessons learned in step 5 not only foster dialogue and force cross-functional communication, they also help us to see risk holistically.

Exercise: Lessons Learned

What have you learned from your organisation's mistakes and the risks you have undertaken?

The Risk Audit

Effectively managing the risk of doing business is becoming a critical driver in many companies' success or failure. Taking a comprehensive view of your risk management strategies periodically through an audit or formal review process is a good way to learn from your successes and misses. This risk management review is an opportunity for the company to assess its ability to both handle risk and to recover from its downside. The key element is to make sure that you are actually learning something so you see improvement over time. For example, an acquisition, a merger, or the significant change in accounting policy within the company can significantly change your organisation's risk strategy.

Ongoing Protection

Think of managing a risk as protecting your personal computer from a virus. A virus can come through many different forms. So you establish a firewall to prevent viruses from coming through your ISP. But do not forget that viruses can be attached to documents that are in purchased software or when someone gets into a computer system through an employee's unprotected home terminal. Even worse, someone could send you what seems to be a harmless E-card that contains a virus which is not detected by your firewall. Even if you have the best firewall available, you must update it regularly and run a daily check for new viruses to make sure that the tool is doing its job.

The same holds true for your risk management programme. You could have strategies and tools in place, but that will not always prevent a costly risk from affecting you, especially if it comes from left field, like one caused by a foreign government or by a strategic partner who has nothing to do with you. Just as you update your firewall and run a daily protection scan, you must also regularly review your risk program by updating your strategies, examining your plans, and conducting a risk audit or review.

A risk audit will help you to know if your risk management programme stays in alignment with your company's overall strategy and objectives. The goal is to make risk management review a part of your everyday business. You can use this review process to strengthen long-term relationships (and hopefully reduce premiums) with insurance brokers and underwriters.

As you gather information from your periodic risk audit, this information will be helpful in negotiating with underwriters. Resist the temptation to tie the timing of this review to the purchase of your insurance. The goal of the review is to identify the weaknesses in your system of controls regarding risk identification, oversight, and mitigation. More than likely, you will find in your review that your company has retained a certain risk unintentionally, either through benign neglect or lack of internal communication.

Risk Audit Team

Your audit team consists of people throughout the organisation, including operations, accounting, IT, human resources, and any other service areas that are affected by risks such as a safety programme. It is critical that this cross-functional team communicate and relate well with each other, because their charter is to ask one another: "What is keeping you awake at night beyond our ordinary risks?" This requires the team to think creatively and organically, and look holistically at the business. If applied properly, the annual review will open employees' eyes to the impact that one risk could have on multiple departments or functions within the business.

This audit team must be headed by a senior executive who represents both the company and shareholders' interests as they relate to risk management. The goal of the committee is to develop a customised audit risk checklist so that individual managers (the actual risk takers) can assess the risk versus reward of their particular area of responsibility. The checklist asks managers to indicate their awareness and knowledge of the potential risks, define those risks, and identify how they are being addressed on an everyday basis. The critical question could be: "How many resources are being spent to address or mitigate this issue?" Do not forget that the resources include people's time, extra paperwork, audits, and energy—the time that could be spent in more productive endeavours.

The Audit's Findings

When the risk review is complete, your company's next step is to use the information that it gathers to improve its overall risk management. By incorporating the review's findings into a specific plan for risk management, the company should be able to minimise the chance that the audit findings will gather dust on your shelf. It makes sense that the leader of this audit team is the chief risk officer, and part of the team's membership consists of members from the risk management committee.

Your risk audit will likely provide you with a great deal of knowledge about your current state of affairs as it relates to risk management and your overall state of risk taking. Some of this knowledge will be beneficial and welcome, while other parts of it will be dreaded and unwelcome. In risk management, knowing the good with the bad makes the organisation stronger and more likely to withstand serious and unanticipated risk. It may even give you a competitive advantage and build the confidence to risk more.

Tool for Continuous Learning

The Plus/Delta analysis tool (figure 8-1) is an excellent learning tool for every meeting, project, or performance evaluation.

Figure 8-1 The Plus/Delta Tool	
<u>Pluses +</u> (Things that work and should be kept)	<u>Deltas Δ</u> (Things that need to change or be better)

The Plus/Delta analysis is a summary of what is worth repeating and what needs improving. It spawns rapid improvements, shortens the learning curve, and increases accountability.

The Plus/Delta gives employees and the risk audit team invaluable insight on what to continue doing and what to change. They use this as they plan for each risky venture, during the progress and monitoring, and at the end. At each phase, the things that are working are identified (pluses) and the improvements noted.

Steps of the Plus/Delta:

1. Announce the purpose of the Plus/Delta.
2. Spend time gathering a list of things that worked well and list them on the "plus" side.

3. Spend time gathering a list of things that people would like to see changed and list them on the "delta" side.

4. Before the next session or committee meeting, address the changes that were recommended and accommodate those that cannot be changed.

5. Start the next meeting by reviewing the most recent Plus/Delta.

6. Remind the group that you will continue doing what worked.

7. Inform the group of the changes that will come from the list.

8. Explain which changes cannot be implemented, and brainstorm alternatives.

9. Continue to use the Plus/Delta tool at each meeting, event, or gathering.

10. Notice and celebrate how quickly improvements are taking place.

Case Study

Analysis of Mega-Retailer's Growing Risk

Despite its decades of success, Mega-Retailer is a very large target for many. For instance, a union-backed group has set a goal of reforming the company's stance on business, labour, environmental, and social standards. Mega-Retailer is also being pressured by local governments to improve its employees' health benefits. After some bad publicity, Mega-Retailer has put its CEO on a national speaking tour and has increased the money it spends trying to influence legislators' policy decisions.

The lesson here is that even if you are a success, you run the risk of people and organisations resenting your success or expecting something of you that they believe you owe them. This same phenomenon has happened to Sainsbury's, Starbucks, Mitsubishi Electric, Heineken Holding, and others. This sadly will continue indefinitely. This risk is both uninsurable and very difficult to quantify and measure.

CEO Lessons Learned

Even bold risk takers realise they cannot foresee every pitfall or downside:

- Richard Branson of Virgin Atlantic—"I wanted to be an editor or journalist, I wasn't really interested in being an entrepreneur, but I soon found I had to become an entrepreneur in order to keep my magazine going."

- Gerry Harvey of Harvey Norman Holdings Limited—"...the customer determines at the end of the day who is successful and for what reason."

- Nikki Strange of DriveSavers—"People's fear and frustration about losing data prevents them from thinking clearly. As long as the anger is 'out-there' blaming others, it prevents quick recovery."

- Andrew Jarecki, CEO of MovieFone—"We failed to test the system before implementing a high-tech solution in a low-tech environment."

- Orit Gadiesh, Chairman of Bain and Company—"We rushed implementation of a client project."

- Barry Keesan, CEO of WorkSmart International—"We undercapitalised an expansion of a fast-growing publishing business."

- Ingvar Kamprad, founder of IKEA—"Only those who are asleep make no mistakes."

Summary: The Importance of Step 5

This step, a healthy evolution in a business, is maturity. In the prior steps, we acknowledged that the downside of risk taking exists and that it is inevitable. Now that we have this realisation, employees have tools that they can use to learn from successes and failures. As in the example given about protecting your personal computer from viruses, a risk management programme provides a firewall for the organisation as a whole.

9

Step Five½—Commit to Taking Action

After reading this chapter, you should be able to

- rate your risk management programme against a continuous improvement environment.
- create an action plan that addresses areas of risk within your firm.
- obtain written commitment from employees on what they will actually do to minimise or address unnecessary risk.

The (Never Completed) Last Step

To you, this last step may seem like an afterthought, yet it is very crucial to the success of your risk planning efforts. Even if we learn something from our lessons learned programme (in step 5), unless your employees actually implement the identified changes and improvements, you waste the time spent in understanding the causes of risks and how to avoid them. Almost every organisation that has an effective risk management programme, especially those that have implemented enterprise risk management protocols, believes that risk management becomes a natural part of its continuous improvement culture.

Familiarize yourself with the term *continuous improvement*, which means that we are constantly working to improve what we are doing. This strive-for-quality attitude includes streamlining processes, rethinking work, re-evaluating every goal, and eliminating unnecessary work and waste; all designed to make things better and lower the cost of doing business. This cultural norm must be included in an effective risk management programme. If it is absent, your people will continue to take the same needless risks again and again.

New or improved courses of action will arise from the cross-functional team approach of looking at risk. The chief risk officer (or focal point for your risk management program) is the person responsible for ensuring that each member of the risk management team commits to implementing the changes and improvements that have been identified and quantified.

Some organisations have turned this chief risk officer role over to the internal audit department, as was previously discussed. Whether it is considered to fit as a function of internal audit or a function of the risk management team, this group must constantly seek out improvement that could potentially lead to better risk evaluation techniques and more tools for employees to use. And this group must end weaknesses in strategies, identify metrics, establish goals, and instil rewards. In fact, the risk management team will end up monitoring your firm's culture mosaic.

It is essential to make sure your plan emphasises and obtains firm commitments from employees who are responsible to be on the lookout for the conditions that lead to unnecessary or costly risk.

Action Plan: Tool for Planning for Risks

The tool that is best used for this step is the formalised action plan. An action plan is a visual definition or map of what it will take to make significant progress on a specific objective.

The payoff from using formalised action plans is their ability to communicate accountability to people.

The contents of an action plan include the following:

- Overall strategic objective
- Deliverables and due dates
- Major steps
- Detailed steps
- Individual responsibilities
- Anticipated obstacles and challenges
- Performance metrics

Your action plan should define each level of change responsibility at the outset. Action plan participants include the following:

Sponsor. Person who has the ability to pay for the change and has ultimate accountability.

Advocate. Person who drives, wants, or demands the change.

Customer. Person who benefits from the change.

Agent of change. Person who carries the responsibility for facilitating the change.

Accountability partner. Person who will help to hold the change agent's feet to the fire; not quite a mentor, the change agent regularly reports back to this person about the progress (or lack of) made toward the plan's end state.

What the action plan tool is for:

- Highlighting overall objectives
- Showing expected or desired results
- Keeping track of actual results
- Holding employees to task
- Identifying risks in advance

A sample strategic action plan is illustrated as figure 9-1.

Figure 9-1
Strategic Action Plan

A Strategic Action Plan or Initiative

Overall Strategic Goal: Dispose of obsolete and dropped inventory products profitably.

Measurable Strategic Plan Tactic: Reduce inventory by 20% and improve the turnover from 4 turns to 6 turns.

Connection to our risk management programme:

In the company's risk management plan, we've addressed the concern that as a new company, we have not established sufficient protocols and controls to deal with obsolete inventories. We acknowledged in the risk management plan that we are in the negative cash flow position currently and will be for the next 18 months. Therefore, our inherent risk is that we may focus too much attention on managing cash, accounts receivable, and accounts payable and not enough attention on the balance sheet items unrelated to immediate cash flows.

Major Action Steps:

1. *Implement a plan to dispose of all aged inventory.*
2. *Implement a plan to dispose of all dropped products.*
3. *Establish controls to ensure the old and obsolete products are sold for their highest value.*
4. *Establish a way to provide an incentive for a sales employee to sell old products without hurting the sales of current products.*

Anticipated Obstacles and Challenges:

1. *Assigning the responsibilities to sell and ship the products to an already overworked staff.*
2. *Finding an inexpensive way to move inventory from the Ohio warehouse to the buyer.*
3. *Protecting the company's reputation, while disposing of obsolete products.*
4. *Convincing our suppliers to take back some products and issue credits.*
5. *Paying adequate incentive compensation to employees who sell the inventory, because there will be no profit margin to the company.*
6. *Determining the negative financial impact of the disposal and communicating this to the board and the bank.*
7. *Keeping the momentum needed to fully dispose of all obsolete products.*

Detailed Activities:

1. *Select the products for disposal (see SKU reduction plan).*
2. *Have the purchasing manager provide an analysis of the returnability of the dropped products.*
3. *Contact any companies who buy products like ours in bulk.*
4. *Hire a telemarketing person to handle the sale of smaller quantities.*
5. *Establish a commission or incentive plan for obsolete product sales.*
6. *Determine the approval levels for authorising the sale price.*
7. *Prepare weekly updates and the status of sales and negotiations.*

Change Team:

Change Agents:
Sponsor:
Champion:

Tool for Action Plan Reporting and Accountability

Figures 9-2 and 9-3 are sample forms that help capture both action plan reporting and accountability within an organisation.

Figure 9-2
Action Plan Reporting Tool

Action Plans Summary

Employees Involved	Action Plan's Strategic Goal	Expected Financial Results		Actual Results	
		Increased Sales $$	(Decreased) Expenses $$	Financial **as of April 30, 2008**	Non-Financial **as of April 30, 2008**
Sponsor—Ron R. Advocate—the Board Customers—Purchasing, Sales Agents—Ron, Keith, Donovan, Bob M.	Dispose of obsolete and dropped inventory products profitably	$5,000	$7,580		
Sponsor— Advocate— Customers— Agent—					
Sponsor— Advocate— Customers— Agent—					
Sponsor— Advocate— Customers— Agent—					

Definitions:

Sponsor— the person who has the ability to pay for the change.

Advocate—the person who wants or demands the change.

Customers—the recipients who benefit from the change.

Agents —the persons responsible for facilitating the change.

Figure 9-3
Personal Commitment Form

Tool for Obtaining Commitment

Activity: What Is Your Next Step?

It is now your turn to do something to improve your own results. Please complete the following:

1.   Using the information I now have, I will use it for

2.   Using the information I have practiced, I will continue to become more comfortable by

3.   Using what I have learned, I will help my organisation or co-workers by

4.   I specifically need the following to be successful:

       Coach_____

       Mentor_____

       Specific training_____

       More support_____

5.   I commit to taking these actions, and I will check back with myself to verify that I have done something on or around _____ (follow-up date).

       Date prepared_____

       My signature_____

       My accountability partner is_____

       I will check in with my accountability partner every _____ days.

Summary: The Importance of Step 5½

There is an old saying about the job not being complete until the paperwork is done. You can make the same case for your risk management plan. The plan is not executed until you see employees incorporate it into their daily behaviours. This is why this final (never completed) step is the bookend to step 1, where we define what risk is at a global level. Now to ensure that our risk plan works, we must move it down to risk at the individual level. This last step is accomplished by holding people accountable to what they commit to doing regarding the awareness, analysis, measurement, and management of risks undertaken.

10

Risk Management and the Management Accountant

After reading this chapter, you should:

- recognise the impact that risk management is having on the accounting profession.
- add value to the discussion of risk for your clients or your employer.
- be able to use your understanding of the path of least resistance principle to isolate inherent and detection risk.

The Demand for Our Risk Awareness

As auditors and business advisors, we must recognise that our role includes providing assurance that controls are in place, and thus detect and monitor problems.

In the accounting profession, we place these risks into three categories:

- Inherent risk
- Control risk
- Detection risk

Most businesses do somewhere between a good to an adequate job of addressing their control risk. Internal controls, internal audits, and the like help leaders and boards of directors examine the checks and balances that need to be in place to hold people accountable.

Yet, breaches of ethics and rash decision-making occur most often because accounting firms and their clients' leaders fail to adequately address the first and third risks. Why? Because we also follow the path of least resistance and focus too much attention on control risk.

Inherent Risk

Inherent risk is the susceptibility of a leader's assertion to a material omission or misstatement. The risk of such an omission or falsehood is greater for some assertions and types of transactions than for others. The primary cause of inherent risk may be both from internal and external sources. An example of inherent risk is the business model for developing commercial buildings that are built on specifications. This means the builder must anticipate what the yet-to-be-identified purchaser might want in a commercial building. The inherent risks the developer faces in his business model are as follows:

- Tying up huge amounts of capital for long periods of time
- Mistiming the market for commercial property
- Dealing with regional economic conditions
- Changing trends in what commercial tenants want in their buildings
- Revising a nearly completed building to suit a new tenant

Control Risk

This is the risk that something material (quite large and significant) will be omitted or misstated and yet will not be prevented or detected in a timely manner. An example is where inventory in an offsite storage locker is not counted and no one notices. This means that the control designed to ensure that we count all inventory is at risk because it failed, and we did not detect the mistake.

Assertion

Whenever you state that something is true, you assert to its truth. In a company's financial statement, the CEO and CFO assert that the data and numbers in it are accurate to the best of their knowledge.

Detection Risk

Detection risk is the risk that the firm's employee, making an assertion, did not uncover or find a material omission or misstatement that exists in his or her statement about the accuracy or correctness.

Detection risk is a function of both the effectiveness and application of an audit or testing process on the area at risk. The employee or auditor looking for detection risk can control it by carefully selecting and applying audit tests to the area. For example, at one company employees perpetuated a fraud of recording expenses as assets by making their entries under $29,999. They knew the external auditors only looked at capital asset transactions over $30,000.

Risk management principle 10:

- Identifying risks in advance determines the likelihood that you will find the conditions that give rise to the risk

---

Risk and Path of Least Resistance

Why do people naturally take the path of least resistance?
The path of least resistance is the principle that energy moves where it is easiest for it to go. It is a reality that a person will frequently take the course that is the most convenient or least painful.

The first thing an auditor and the CFO or controller must understand is the path of least resistance (POLR) principle. To do this, you need to study human behaviour and be on constant vigilance for places that the POLR can exist. By discovering POLR for undesirable behaviours, you can easily shape behaviours to better ones. We can better understand the POLR with these truisms.

Risk management principles 11–13:

- When I display a behaviour that increases risk, it is usually because my behaviour is the path of least resistance. There is some sort of payoff for my actions.
- Temptations to take the path of least resistance come in many forms, and you're not aware of most them.
- If I chose to shape your behaviour, I need to alter the existing path of least resistance

---

Answer these questions:

Why does the POLR principle show up in the workplace?

How does the POLR arise when there are no rules or guidelines for employees regarding risk taking?

How does the POLR arise when there are specific written rules or guidelines for employees regarding risk taking?

Where Auditors Need to Look

Client's Rewards

The actions and decisions that leaders reward tell employees what is most important. People pay attention to who is rewarded and why. If employees are rewarded for the wrong behaviours, other people see this and model those same behaviours. If a negative behaviour is displayed by an employee and the action is either ignored or condoned, other employees see this and ignore the behaviour or model it.

Often, auditors will examine the formalised reward system of their clients, but they fail to investigate the informal rewards. This habit especially affects accounting departments because most accounting teams are in the business of catching other people's errors. We also see this as our sworn duty; we fix the error and rarely do something about the cause. In effect, when we do this, the accounting department and the firm's leaders have rewarded the behaviours that fostered the error in the first place.

Here are some questions to regularly ask of those whom you are auditing or supervising:

- Could someone who is in a position of power get away with a detrimental behaviour?
- Why does this firm have or need rewards?
- What are employees being rewarded for?
- What form do they take?
- What sorts of messages do the formal rewards send?
- How are these positively aimed rewards being subverted?

Internal Pressures

Pressures to perform have the same impact on taking risks as rewards—and employees are almost always under some pressure to perform. In fact, the greater the need for the firm to take risks and the higher the rewards are for being innovative, the greater the likelihood for undue pressure placed on employees to achieve certain results exists.

There is a delicate balance between the incentive to achieve something and the pressure to perform. Applying pressure to achieve can be a positive tool that is often subverted. For example, the CEO may request that the sales group provide him with stretch numbers. If sales are higher than the original target, the sales team earns rewards or extra money. This incentive crosses the line to the bad side when the pressure is great but the employee lacks the tools or the means to achieve the higher target or is penalised for achieving the originally acceptable target.

There is a corollary to the POLR principle regarding incentives and rewards: if employees are shown a large carrot, yet cannot achieve it through legitimate means, and the carrot is something that they must have (to keep their job or pay the rent) the employee will almost always find a way to get the carrot. The means an employee uses may not always be justified.

This corollary is often where unnecessary risk and unethical actions start: the pressure to perform combined with an incentive to perform combined with the inability to perform.

Here are some questions to ask yourself as you prepare to look for inherent risk:

- Do employees see a difference between a stretch goal and an unrealistic goal?
- Are employees required to explain the means to a predefined end?
- Are employees held accountable for how they achieve their goals, or just for achieving them?
- Where do pressures to perform or achieve a specific result come from, and why do they exist?
- How do employees typically respond to performance pressures?
- How do employees respond if the pressure is excessive or if the goal is unrealistic?

Ways to Alter Employee's Path of Least Resistance

- Limit the choices or options
- Eliminate all other possibilities so that one choice remains

  The more choices employees have, the more likely that they will take the path that you may not approve of or recommend.

- Focus on the process instead of the result

  As described earlier, we have to hold people accountable for how they get the results as well as for achieving the results.

- Clarify and change the default choice
- Impose preconditions on each choice

  While we want employees to think for themselves, we also want to ensure that they think through each of their decisions before acting rashly or unwisely. Leaders need to model for their employees the default choice and explain to employees the real impact for each of the available options.

- Make the obvious choice the one with least pain or most pleasure.

  Setting rewards for achievement is good and so is establishing penalties for lack of achievement. Whenever you use the carrot to induce good behaviour, ensure that employees know there is a stick on the other end to encourage the good behaviour.

- Make the choice by consensus

  The more people included in a decision, the more likely you will discover the risk and downside of each choice. Three heads are truly better than one.

11

The Wide World of Risks

After reading this chapter, you should

- understand that risk comes in many forms and from many sources.
- be able to use this information to broaden your risk management plan.
- find many useful risk mitigation ideas.

Risk in Weather

Today the weather has become a major risk. Look at the effects of the Icelandic volcano Grimsvötn, and the impact on businesses and their employees in the United Kingdom and Europe. One strategy you can pursue to minimise the risk and cost of weather-related incidents is reviewing your insurance coverage.

Risk in Geopolitics

Even violence from events that are unrelated to your business can spill over to your organisation; therefore, you must have a response plan to address them if they occur. We saw an example of this risk in Zurich during the World Trade Organization demonstrations in 2009.

Due to globalisation, leaders of organisations need to face up to political risk. You may not have physical locations outside your country, but your customer base, your distribution channel, or even your main suppliers could immediately be out of commission or subject to huge costs for doing business in some nations. Countries around the world have political leaders who feel that it is their right to change the rules in the middle of the game. Companies doing business in foreign markets also face up to the risk over the confiscation or appropriation of their property, politically motivated violence, and the problems of managing local currency.

As you can see, the ways that the company evaluates or perceives risk can have a great impact on how it puts together its business model. Every company will continue to face new challenges it cannot predict adequately. However, a comprehensive risk management plan with specific proactive methodology for identifying, assessing, quantifying, and mitigating risks increases your confidence in dealing with geopolitical issues that might involve your firm either directly or indirectly.

Risk From People Resources

Risk From Fraud and Employee Abuses

The overall loss from fraud is estimated to be over $660 billion or 6% of revenues. Fraud and abuse translates into $9 per day per employee.

How many employees work in your organisation? _____

Multiply that number times $9 times 365. This figure will give you a compelling reason to be concerned about breaches in ethics in your organisation.

White-collar fraud continues to grow. The 2004 *Report on Occupational Fraud and Abuse* from the Association of Certified Fraud Examiners (ACFE) provided an estimate that the highest losses from white-collar fraud—46%—occur in businesses of fewer than 100 employees. These are the businesses that are less likely to have audits or have strong cultures of ethics.

Fraud is a crime based on concealment, and many organisations do not know that they are being victimised. Occupational fraud ranges from simple stealing of company assets to complex financial manipulation. Most frauds are either never detected or go on for years before they are discovered.

Small businesses are more vulnerable to breaches in ethics due to three factors:

1. They are less likely to require an audit.
2. They do not have a hotline for employees to report breaches.
3. They rarely have adequate internal controls.

One of the most common forms of fraud is kickbacks or conflicts of interest involving employees and others. Other forms of business fraud include the following:

- Fraudulent disbursements
- Skimming (cash stolen before the company has recorded it)
- Larceny (cash stolen after the company has recorded it)
- Fraudulent billings to fictitious companies or for fictitious goods or services
- Employees making false claims for compensation
- Employees requesting reimbursement for fictitious or inflated expenses

The CFE study estimates that 75% of all cash frauds come in the form of fraudulent disbursements.

Hotlines will not always bring frauds to light, but they do create a reporting mechanism for employees that allows for the collection of tips on possible wrongdoing. Firms that use such a hotline are more likely to be aware of potential frauds by employees but also by customers, vendors, and third parties. Firms that utilise employee hotlines or some sort of anonymous and safe reporting mechanism show the greatest decrease in actual frauds. A critical element in almost every discovered fraud is a dishonest employee who had the opportunity to commit the infraction.

What is most interesting is that the CFE survey found that over half the frauds committed by an owner or executive were detected through an anonymous tip.

More CFE findings were that

- only 6% of the frauds were caught via the firm's internal controls.
- 33% of frauds in small business involve a billing scheme.
- 33% of frauds involved check alteration.
- 82% of fraud cases were asset theft.

Finally, the CFE study concluded that for the small businesses included in the study, only 31% had any form of internal audit or fraud examination department.

Those surveyed in the study gave their opinions about today's business environment:

- 67% say that fraud is worse today than five years ago.
- 70% say fraud detection is getting better.
- 75% say fraud detection resources are not adequate.

The CFE's 2004 study's results are consistent with those of its 2002 study.

Warning Signs of Situations at Risk for Unethical Behaviours

The following make up the 80% of people who would defraud you if they could and the 10% that will anyway.

- Employees who are being downsized
- Employees who are bored and looking for excitement
- Employees who find a hole in the company's internal controls, benefit from it, and do not report the lapse
- Employees who enjoy bending the rules
- Employees who are under personal stress
- Employees who experience personal financial problems or setbacks
- Employees with addictions, such as alcohol or gambling
- Employees who need to be the centre of attention

Even by the standards of recent fraud statistics, the 70% increase in staff deception reported by CIFAS, the UK's Fraud Prevention Service, for the year to June 2009 was an eye opener. And there is no reason to anticipate an imminent reversal.

UK unemployment is at its highest level for 14 years and still rising. The correlation between periods of economic downturn and certain types of criminal activity including theft and fraud is well established. In the latest example, the UK has just become the shoplifting capital of Europe with nearly £5 billion worth of goods disappearing off retailer shelves over the last year. Of this figure, 36% was attributed to employee theft.

Australia's Carbon Pollution Reduction Scheme (CPRS) will soon require the largest emitters of greenhouse gases to offset their carbon footprint. Such schemes have already been subject to fraud, misstatement and the involvement of organised crime in the UK and Europe. Deloitte Forensic is now warning Australian companies and regulators to prepare for the potential fraud risks.

Risk in Your Static Rewards

Behaviour never remains static. As a leader you must be willing to alter your visible and invisible reward systems, your compensation systems, your people systems, and your communication systems whenever employees show behaviours that diminish the ethics of your organisation.

Change your compensation system and employees will automatically change their behaviour. The job of the twenty-first century leader is to drive desired behaviour and model the high standards of the organisation.

Risk in Employment Compliance

Another area to address in your risk management plan is compliance with worker health and safety regulations, as well as laws against employment discrimination. As with all regulations, it is difficult for companies to keep up, yet expensive if they are unable to comply with the latest changes. Business leaders continue to use downsizing or rightsizing, but this competitive tool has a huge negative impact on the employees who lose their jobs and livelihoods. Terminations may turn into a situation in which disgruntled employees exact revenge. Previous cases of such outbursts have been triggered by mergers or downsizing. Your company should pay very close attention to your people problems of all magnitude and to employees' emotional states which arise from these difficult situations.

Risk in the Technology Dependent Age

Risk in Information Security

In today's world, we all rely heavily on our computers and a wide range of technology. This progress puts all of our firms in an extremely vulnerable position because we are only as good or as secure as our information security systems. The following are some examples of where today's dangers or risks in information security occur:

- Airborne assaults from electronics such as a smart phone or a personal digital assistant
- Anti-websites set up to defame your company
- Attacks in networks linking home and business computers
- Children's access to technology
- Corporate spies
- Cyber smearing
- Cyber terrorists
- Disgruntled employees
- Electrical blackouts (local, regional, or national)
- Foreign intelligence
- Frauds, such as phishing
- Hackers and crackers
- Hidden cameras in bathrooms and changing rooms placed there by employers or others
- Organised crime groups
- Legitimate websites hijacked for pornography purposes
- System cracking through server computers where legitimate websites are housed
- Spyware
- Targeted mass postings of worms and viruses or Trojan horses
- URL squatters who look for prominent sites for which the owners have not renewed the registration
- WiFi systems and wireless networks

Answer this question:

How many technology risks have you included in your firm's risk management strategy or risk portfolio?

Information that is leaked outside the organisation can have an impact on the company's fortunes, plans, reputation, and marketing efforts. Inadequate patent protection of your inventions can cost you your competitive edge and potential profits. As a leader, you must be proactive in protecting every single piece of sensitive information from loss or theft. We want this protection 100% of the time, but that would be impossible and incredibly expensive. For example, a typical office desk is a virtual gold mine of sensitive information. One outsider rifling through your employees' desks could find tremendous information that could be valuable to someone outside your organisation.

It is imperative that leaders ensure that every employee understands the nature of sensitive information and incorporate proactive protection and security training into your everyday basic security techniques. Likewise, when an employee who is knowledgeable leaves your organisation, you must do everything you can to secure both the company information and sensitive data.

E-Commerce Risk

The best approach to addressing risk management today is a proactive stance anticipating your risks and working to keep them from biting your firm. This will help you to prepare for today's fast-paced and global world of business. A thoughtful and proactive strategy prevents or anticipates problems in the first place, creating the need for a formalised risk management programme. An effective risk management plan can help you deal with bad publicity, help reduce insurance costs, and keep your business running smoothly.

E-commerce is changing the business world beyond just an opportunity to generate more revenue. E-commerce affects privacy, security, and intellectual property. The business risks of e-commerce go beyond hackers and network breakdowns because they threaten the very existence of your business and entire market segments. As part of your risk management strategy, you need to assess whether your products could become redundant or obsolete and how your existing sales or delivery methods may be affected by e-commerce.

Risk of Sabotage

We refer to them as "hackers" or "crackers" or worse, but there is a difference. Hackers are in your system for a joyride. Crackers are there for a malicious purpose. They want to steal some information, store content on your server, slip you a virus, access your cash, or make you look stupid in public. Crackers in your system could leave you liable for their handiwork. Some examples include the following:

- Your bank might expect you to pay for credit card losses should a cracker dig into that system.
- Vendors would expect repayment for the products or services that the cracker ordered through your systems.
- Partners could claim damages for intellectual property being disclosed to the wrong parties.
- Shareholders could sue you for losses to their investment.
- Governmental regulators could treat you as incompetent.

Worst of all, your insurance company may decide you were negligent in protecting yourself against crackers and decline to reimburse you for your defensive costs. It can be expensive not to have a risk management programme, especially one designed to look at the risks in the applications and misuse of your technology.

Hackers and crackers have penetrated such organisations across the globe. The cyber-security company McAfee has released a report saying that over the past five years, cyber hackers have broken into the systems of 72 organizations worldwide. Victims of hacking include governments, international organizations, and private companies. According to Reuters, the 72 organizations hacked into include the governments of the United States, Taiwan, India, South Korea, Vietnam, and Canada, as well as international organizations such as the United Nations and the International Olympic Committee.

No one is exempt from where hackers and crackers decide to go.

The odds of any external invasion into your technology systems are smaller than the odds of someone within your organisation accessing and exploiting your resources. Far more likely risks include the following:

- A disgruntled employee
- A cleaning crew member who rifles through someone's desk
- A bookkeeper who creates a false vendor
- A supplier who is in collusion with your product manager
- An employee who is pulling racist or sexist jokes from the Web and passing them on

A crime or fraud instigated from the inside or outside will very likely be committed using computers. In every organisation and in every industry, it is inevitable.

Small businesses can take some comfort in this: the greater the potential loss, the greater the chance of crime. This means that a cracker may have more opportunity to benefit from invading Vodafone than from invading the local grocery store. This does not mean, however, that you are free from being concerned about these sorts of risks. An invasion or misuse of your firm's computer system can lead to financial devastation. This places risk squarely in the lap of the executive team. Hackers and crackers are persistent and as adaptive as cockroaches and will always be trying to get into your organisation.

Sabotage Mitigation

Your solution is to develop an overall strategy and make the decision to mount a cost-effective defence. You must establish a strict prevention policy, then manage and minimise the risk through whatever steps necessary to prevent financial loss or disaster for the misapplication of the company's information systems. This means that all technology risks must be recognised and prioritised, and their impact minimised, in your risk management plan.

Today, information stored in our files and databases is often the company's most valuable asset, yet it may be given very little attention from a security standpoint. Our firm's leaders must prioritise our information assets according to their worth to the business model and to business continuity. They need to pay attention to protecting the information that is most valuable. A loss could be the disappearance of information caused by a virus, or it could be the transfer of information into the wrong hands. Sadly, such transfers of information do not qualify as thefts in some jurisdictions. A loss of your data is just as bad as the serious loss of face to customers, the public, and your shareholders.

A critical part of your risk management programme is a disaster recovery plan that includes recovery of data and dealing with the possibility of secure information going outside your ordinary channels.

Sabotage and vandalism are alive and well and more costly than the theft of information. A total system security model needs to touch every aspect of the organisation, looking for potential threats and identifying the risk factors, including the cost to recover.

Some technology experts believe that almost all acts of information theft and cyber sabotage can be considered inside jobs. That does not mean that the hacker or cracker is a former employee. It does imply that one or more of your employees were lax in the security system that allowed the outsider into your system. This laxness can include the following:

- Not regularly changing passwords
- Using easy-to-identify passwords
- Passwords written down in Rolodexes
- Passwords posted on the walls of an employee's cubicle
- Passwords written on sticky notes posted on the computer screen

The ingenuity of today's cyber crook will challenge your best efforts and intentions. The only effective corporate policy is not one in your procedure manual, but rather an attitude of constant diligence, consistent improvement, and a thoughtful risk management plan.

Risk to Personal Data

The 2002 Cabinet Office Study, which covered the use of false identities and the theft of other people's identities, estimated that crime facilitated by identity fraud cost the UK £1.3 billion per year. The Home Office Identity Fraud Steering Committee completed an exercise to update the Cabinet Office for the purpose of establishing trends in the cost of identity fraud. The latest estimate (February 2006) is that identity fraud costs the UK economy £1.7 billion. People's personal information is not only stored in your firm's computers, it is also contained in your old file cabinets, discarded boxes, and, of course, the landfill. No controls over this data will ever be 100% secure, and every one of us is at risk, especially if your employees use such information in ways that violate your policies. One of the ways that you can protect yourself is to safeguard both your incoming and outgoing mail. Another way is to shred all business documents using a professional and bonded shredding company.

Risk in E-Mail

Spam-related regulations in many countries have defined what organisations can and cannot do with spam. This does not mean that unscrupulous spammers will follow these rules. To help protect your organisation, it is good to not only be aware of these regulations, but to follow them. The scope of the regulations that we all face cover even a single e-mail that you send to a business, partner, or customer.

Risk in Internet Privacy

Privacy on the Internet is a big concern. Consumers are becoming increasingly angry when their personal information is used without their permission. Some regulations have been and will continue to be introduced in order to prevent companies from releasing sensitive customer information to third parties without the consumer's express consent. Consumers are fearful that businesses like yours and its websites are not adequately protected from either an outside invasion or predatory practices by your organisation. Many nations have moved to create guidelines addressed at Internet privacy. A few examples are included below.

U.S. Regulations on Website Risk

In the United States, the protection of an individual's information is governed by laws, court rulings, and self-regulation. Alternatively, certifying organisations (like the American Institute of CPAs or Congress) rely on the members' self-compliance. Here in the United States, the four Fair Information Practices of user security on a website are as follows:

Notice. Give users notice when you are collecting their information and tell them how it will be used and to whom it is disclosed.

Choice. Give users the option of opting out of giving personal information and the option to approve of sharing their information with third parties.

Access. Give the user reasonable access to the information you have on them and give them the ability to correct all erroneous data.

Security. Establish reasonable measures to protect users' data.

European Regulations on Web Site Risk

Passed in 1995, the E.U. Privacy Directive has important implications for both companies engaged in e-commerce and for multinational companies with offices in European countries. The directive is based on the idea that collecting and using personal information infringes upon the fundamental right to privacy and covers a wide variety of data that might be transmitted during the ordinary course of business. Businesses that want to trade in E.U. countries must guarantee that the user's personal data is

- processed fairly and lawfully.
- collected for specified, legitimate purposes.
- accurate and up-to-date.
- kept only for the stated purposes and nothing more.

In addition to the U.S. minimum standards of notice, choice, access, and security, the E.U. directive requires three more user protections:

Onward transfer. You can only disclose user information consistent with your published notice and choice standards.

Data integrity. You must take reasonable steps to ensure that all user data collected is accurate, complete, and current.

Enforcement. You must place mechanisms to give users recourse if a complaint or a dispute arises.

The term *user* refers to individuals, but it would add to your reputation for integrity if your firm applies them to the businesses that visit and use your website.

Worldwide Regulations on Web Site Risk

A number of countries in the Arabic region have already undertaken national measures and adopted approaches to combat cybercrime, or are in the process of drafting legislation. Examples of such countries include Pakistan, Egypt, and the United Arabic Emirates (UAE). In order to harmonise legislation in the region, the UAE submitted model legislation to the Arab League (Guiding Law to Fight IT Crime). In 2003, the Arab Interior Ministers Council and the Arab Justice Ministers Council adopted the law. The Gulf Cooperation Council (GCC) recommended at a conference in 2007 that the GCC countries seek a joint approach that takes into consideration international standards.

The bottom line is that all businesses must take consumer privacy issues seriously. This will require you to invest resources to secure both your internal databases and your website. Your firm's leadership must also determine if your insurance covers lawsuits that may arise over privacy issues. All organisations with an online presence will need to establish online privacy statements certifying that they comply with the current privacy standards in both their country and abroad. Make sure your website and Internet presence is covered in your risk management plan.

Risk of Internet Rumours

The Internet has accelerated the way that the stock market reacts to information both good and bad about companies. A new phenomenon that has grown is called cyber smear. The reasons for cyber smear are sometimes economic profit and personal gain, but they are not exclusively the reason more and more firms and their owners are finding that the Internet can facilitate low cost cyber smear campaigns. In a number of cases, the cyber smear campaign was motivated by revenge. Messages are posted by disgruntled employees or insiders, ex-employees, envious ex-colleagues, competitors, creditors, and even people seeking a forum when they are denied employment with you.

Ways that companies can protect themselves are to monitor stock chat message boards. Other companies are protecting themselves against this risk by hiring third parties that specialise in a service of checking the Internet for cases of potential cyber smear. This protection is expensive but may be worth it the more likely a target you are. A good place to start is by visiting the eWatch website.

Summary: The Importance of These Risks

Do you ever wish to go back to a day when life was simpler? I would bet that we have all entertained such a harmless desire. What is harmful is if you were to attempt to live your life as if life contained no complexity at all. In fact, that could be dangerous. That is why we need to pay attention to the many types of risks contained in this chapter. The likelihood of your firm being subject to all of them is remote. However, if your business is growing and becoming more innovative, risk generated by people in your organisation will be greater.

In an effective risk management plan, as you have discovered, it is important that leaders look globally at all the potential risks that could undermine the firm's success. The more information you have available to you, the more risk savvy you will be. Therefore, knowing that all these possible risks are out there, from organised crime groups to cyber smears and Internet rumours, helps everyone in the organisation to be both wary and aware. These two attitudes, in combination, help employees and leaders become better risk managers.

Appendix A

Tool for Culture Risk Assessment

An amazing tool was developed by Robert Simons, a professor of business administration and director of research at Harvard Business School. Simons' tool, which he calls the risk exposure calculator, helps managers and leaders determine the amount of internal risk to which they expose their businesses. The calculator consists of the following three pressure points.

Pressure Point No. 1: The Growth Factor

Fast growing businesses are intense and exciting, but also create pressures to perform. Fast growth leads us to promoting or hiring inexperienced personnel into key positions. This pressure point, if handled correctly, leads to greater success. However, if handled poorly, it fosters greater risk exposure.

Pressure Point No. 2: The Corporate Culture

The internal workings of the organisation, known as its culture, significantly affect people's approach to viewing risk. Simons identified three specific areas within this pressure point:

- Rewards for entrepreneurial risk taking
- Executive resistance to bad news
- Level of internal competitiveness

Pressure Point No. 3: The Management of Information

A fast-growing organisation must have the ability to obtain timely and accurate feedback. Without this ability, bad news is often late, mislaid or, even worse, transformed into good news. The three concerns of this pressure point are as follows:

- Transaction complexity and velocity
- Gaps in diagnostic performance metrics
- The degree of decentralised decision making

Then, based on how the decision makers view their own organisation, Simons' calculator becomes self-rating. Organisations with low scores are in the *safety zone*. Companies with medium scores are in the *caution zone*. Firms with the highest scores are in the *danger zone*. Simons' tested his risk exposure calculator on hundreds of different companies that attended Harvard Business School's executive education programmes.

Simons' tool then asks five questions that help managers understand the relationship between risk and reward. He helps managers to see that they have four levers that they can use to control risk as their company pursues its specific strategy. The four areas he identified as levers are as follows:

1. The firm's belief systems
2. The firm's boundary systems
3. The firm's diagnostic control systems
4. The firm's interactive control systems

Working together, these four levers give managers and executives the tools to balance profits and growth with control. Each of these levers must be carefully aligned with the firm's global strategy.

Simons next asks executives to answer these five questions. As a whole, the answers create awareness about their firm's control environment over risk management:

- Question 1—*Have your senior managers communicated the core values of the business in a way that people understand and embrace?*
- Question 2—*Have your leaders clearly identified the specific actions and behaviours that are off limits?*
- Question 3—*Are your diagnostic control systems adequate at monitoring critical performance variables?*
- Question 4—*Are your control systems interactive and designed to stimulate learning?*
- Question 5—*Are you paying enough for traditional internal controls?*

The full force of question five forces the executive to see how the leaders value the control systems overall, because, as a company grows, the money invested in the control systems must grow commensurately.

Appendix B

Ethics Focus: Business and Industry

Ethics Overview

Compliance with ethical and professional standards is at the very heart of what it means to be a management accountant. Our profession was founded on the qualities of honesty, trustworthiness, being free of conflicts, doing what is right, and having due and proper support for our work and opinions. In the current environment of expanded responsibilities and transparency, greater liability, and new civil and criminal penalties for failure to meet professional standards, each of us is personally and professionally obliged to know and understand our ethical duties. Individual governments and international organizations are committed to increasing awareness of ethical issues and assisting professionals in implementing and sustaining the high ideals of our profession.

Studies have shown that management's demonstrated commitment to ethical behaviour means far more to employees than codes of conduct and training programmes. How do you demonstrate this commitment? By setting the proper tone at the top, fostering the development of an ethical corporate culture, and reinforcing positive organisational values. This means you and your company's senior executives need to take part in implementing ethical standards, enforcing these standards, and providing positive feedback in response to actions that support an ethical environment. Whether you are the CFO or an entry level staff accountant, keep in mind that your actions both form a part of your business's value set and reflect on you and others in the organisation.

Key Ethical Dilemmas

Management accountants in industry face special and unique challenges in fulfilling their ethical responsibilities, particularly because they are accountable to multiple constituencies. Caught between the board of directors, audit committee, outside auditors, internal audit personnel, stockholders, and regulators, industry management accountants can find themselves being pulled in countless directions. Because more than 80% of fraudulent financial reporting has historically originated with the CEO or CFO of a business, pressures on industry management accountants from higher-ups in the organisation can create intolerable situations or even force life-changing decisions. When faced with these circumstances, you need to make the right choice—not the easiest choice or the most expedient. Let us review a few of the more common ethical dilemmas that you may run into as a management accountant.

Integrity and Objectivity

- If I am uncomfortable with disclosure or an entry in the financials, but I have been overruled by my superior, what should I do? Do I have to do anything?

- To what extent am I responsible for preparing our financials in accordance with governing accounting and business practice principles?

- I've heard that when prosecuting employees involved in financial frauds, the government has dealt more harshly with management accountants accused of wrongdoing. Why is that? What does this fact mean to me?

Reporting and Disclosure Protocols

- How far can materiality be taken when applying judgements to financial reporting? What policies and procedures should I apply to enhance the quality of our reporting?

- If my company uses the rollover approach in analysing financial statement misstatements, what is my obligation when considering materiality issues?

- I have become aware of an internal control deficiency—now what?

- Our company engaged a private investigator who is using subterfuge to gain access to phone records of customers and suppliers, and I've become aware of this. What are my professional responsibilities to my employer? What should I do now?

- What are the professional standards that apply to management accountants when making estimates and judgements? What disclosure protocols need to be followed when discussing estimates?

Independence and Due Care

- As an employee, I am not independent—am I still bound by independence concepts?

- As an industry management accountant, what is my supervisory responsibility for others?

- I supervise the tax function at our company. Do I have any special obligations in that position?

Confidentiality

- When does my duty to be candid with the outside auditor override my duty of confidentiality to my employer?

Nonattest Services and Relations With External Auditors

- What approvals must we get for nonattest services from our audit firm? From whom?

- Can we hire someone from our outside audit firm without impairing its independence?

- Our company is interested in getting advice on an aggressive tax shelter that's been proposed to us by a third party. Can we discuss the shelter with our audit firm?

- Our audit firm has always helped us out by preparing the CFO, controller, and assistant controller's personal tax returns. Can they still do this without impairing independence?

Glossary of Controllership and Financial Management Terms

absorption costing. A costing method that treats all manufacturing costs (direct materials, direct labour, variable overhead, and fixed overhead) as product costs. It is also referred to as full costing.

accept or reject decision. Decision resulting from a relevant cost analysis concerning whether to accept or reject a special order.

accounts payable turnover ratio. A liquidity measure that shows the number of times on average that accounts payable are paid during the period; calculated by dividing net credit purchases by average accounts payable during the period.

accounts receivable turnover ratio. A liquidity measure that shows the number of times on average that accounts receivable are collected during the period; calculated by dividing net credit sales by average accounts receivable during the period.

action analysis report. A report detailing the costs that have been assigned to a cost object, such as a product or a customer; it also shows how difficult it would be to adjust the cost if there were a change in activity.

activity. An event that causes the consumption of overhead resources within an organisation.

activity cost pool. A "bucket" in which costs that relate to a single activity measure are accumulated within an activity-based costing system.

activity measure. An allocation basis within an activity-based costing system which, under ideal conditions, measures the amount of activity that drives the costs in an activity cost pool.

activity-based costing (A BC). A costing method that focuses on individual activities as primary cost objects and uses the costs of these activities as the basis for assigning costs to other cost objects, such as products and services.

activity-based management (A BM). A management approach that focuses on managing activities as a way of eliminating waste, reducing delays, and minimising defects.

administrative cost. Any executive, organisational, and clerical cost associated with the general management of an organisation.

average age of inventory. The number of days on average that a company holds inventory before it is sold; calculated by dividing 365 days by the inventory turnover ratio.

average collection period. The number of days on average that an account receivable remains outstanding; calculated by dividing 365 days by the accounts receivable turnover ratio.

average payment period. The number of days on average that an account payable remains unpaid; calculated by dividing 365 days by the accounts payable turnover ratio.

balanced scorecard. An integrated set of financial, customer, internal business processes, and learning and growth performance measures that is derived from and supports an organisation's strategy.

benchmarking. A study of organisations considered to be among the best in performing a particular task. Involves establishment, through data gathering, of targets and comparators, through whose use relative levels of performance can be identified.

bottleneck. Any machine or other part of a process that limits the total output of an entire system.

break-even point. The level of sales, in units or dollars, where profit is zero. It can also be defined as the point where total sales equals total fixed and variable costs, or the point where total contribution margin equals total fixed costs.

budget. A detailed plan for the future acquisition and use of financial and other resources over a specified period of time, usually expressed in formal quantitative terms.

business process. The series of steps followed when carrying out some task in a business.

capital budgeting. The process of planning significant outlays on projects that have long-term implications, such as the acquisition of new property and equipment or the introduction of a new product line.

finance lease. A long-term agreement that allows one party (the lessee) to use the asset of another party (the lessor) in an arrangement accounted for like a purchase.

cash budget. A detailed plan showing the primary sources and uses of cash resources over a specific time period.

cash debt coverage ratio. A measure of solvency that can be calculated by dividing cash provided by operating activities by average total assets.

change management. The process of coordinating a structured period of transition from one situation to another in order to achieve lasting change within an organisation. It can be of varying scope, from continuous improvement to radical and substantial change involving organisational strategy.

chief financial officer (CFO). Top management team member responsible for providing timely and relevant data to support planning and control activities and for preparing financial statements for external users.

committed fixed cost. Any fixed cost that is considered to be difficult to adjust because it relates to the investment in facilities, equipment, or the basic organisational structure of a firm common cost. Costs that are incurred to support a number of costing objects but that cannot be traced to any one of those costing objects individually.

constraint. Any limitation under which an organisation must operate, such as limited available raw materials or machine time, that restricts the organisation's ability to satisfy demand.

contribution margin. The difference between total sales and total variable cost, or the difference between unit selling price and unit variable cost. It represents the amount contributed to covering fixed costs and providing a profit to the organisation.

contribution margin ratio. The ratio of total contribution margin to total sales, or the ratio of unit contribution margin to unit selling price. It is used in cost-volume-profit analysis.

control. The process of establishing procedures and then obtaining feedback in order to ensure that all parts of the organisation are functioning effectively and moving toward overall company goals.

controller. The manager in charge of the organisation's accounting department.

controlling. Ensuring that a plan is actually implemented and appropriately modified as circumstances change.

conversion cost. Costs of converting raw materials into finished goods. It is the sum of direct labour costs plus manufacturing overhead costs.

core competencies. A bundle of skills and technologies that enable a company to provide a particular benefit to customers that gives it competitive differentiation.

corporate governance. The system by which organisations are directed and controlled. Its structure specifies the distribution of rights and responsibilities amongst different participants in the organisation and spells out the rules and procedures for making decisions on corporate affairs. The result is the structure through which corporate objectives are set and through which the means of obtaining those objectives and monitoring performance are achieved.

cost behaviour. How a cost reacts or responds to changes in activity levels. Costs may be fixed, variable, or mixed.

cost centre. A business segment whose manager has control over costs, but not over revenues or the use of invested funds.

cost driver. A factor that causes overhead costs, such as machine hours, labour hours, or computer time.

cost management. The application of managerial accounting concepts, methods of data collection, data analysis, and data presentation so that relevant information can be provided for purposes of planning, monitoring, and controlling costs.

cost object. Anything for which cost data are desired, such as products, product lines, customers, jobs, or organisational subunits.

cost of capital. The average rate of return that a company must pay to its long-term creditors and shareholders for the use of their funds.

cost of goods manufactured. Manufacturing costs associated with goods that are completed and become available for sale during the period.

current cash debt coverage ratio. A measure of liquidity that can be calculated by dividing cash provided by operating activities by average current liabilities.

current ratio. A measure commonly used to evaluate a company's liquidity and short-term debt-paying ability that can be calculated by dividing total current assets by total current liabilities.

customer relationship management. A combination of customer information systems, personalisation systems, content management systems, and campaign management systems.

debt to asset ratio. A measure of solvency that shows the percentage of total assets financed with borrowed funds; calculated by dividing total liabilities by total assets.

decentralisation. The process of delegating decision-making authority throughout an organisation by empowering managers at various operating levels within the organisation to make key decisions relating to their area of responsibility.

depletion. The process of allocating the cost of a natural resource over its estimated useful life.

depletion. The process of allocating the cost of an item of property, plant, and equipment over its estimated useful life.

depreciation. The process of allocating the cost of an intangible asset over its estimated useful life asset turnover rate. The sales divided by the average operating assets figure. It represents the amount of sales generated from each dollar invested in operating assets by an investment centre.

differential cost. Any difference in cost between two alternative courses of action under consideration. Also referred to as relevant cost.

differential revenue. Any difference in revenue between two alternative courses of action under consideration. Also referred to as relevant revenue.

direct allocation method. A method of allocating service department costs to operating departments that allocates all service department costs directly to those operating departments without recognizing any services provided to other service departments.

direct cost. Any cost that can be easily and conveniently traced to a specified cost object.

direct labour. Any manufacturing labour costs that can be conveniently and easily traced to individual units of product.

direct labour budget. A detailed plan that shows the labour requirements needed to meet projected production requirements over a specified period of time.

direct materials. Any manufacturing materials costs that can be conveniently and easily traced to individual units of product.

direct materials budget. A detailed plan that shows the amount of raw materials that must be purchased during a specified period of time in order to meet production needs and provide for the desired level of ending raw materials inventory.

directing. Mobilising employees to carry out plans and perform routine operations.

discretionary fixed cost. Any fixed cost that is considered to be relatively easy to adjust because it arises from annual decisions by management to spend in certain fixed cost areas such as advertising, employee development, or research and development.

duration driver. In activity-based costing, a measure of the amount of time required to perform an activity.

earnings per share (EPS). A measure of the net income earned on each share of ordinary shares outstanding; calculated by dividing net income minus preference shares by the average number of common shares outstanding during the year.

economic value added (EVA). A concept similar to residual income used for performance evaluation purposes.

enterprise governance. The set of responsibilities and practices exercised by executive management and the board of directors with the goal of providing strategic direction, ensuring that objectives are achieved, ascertaining that risks are managed appropriately, and verifying that the organisation's resources are used responsibly. It is wider than, and inclusive of, corporate governance.

feedback. Accounting and non-accounting reports and other information that assist managers in monitoring performance and in focusing on problems or opportunities that might otherwise go unnoticed.

financial accounting. Accounting activities concerned with providing information to external users such as stockholders, creditors, and government agencies.

finished goods. Units of output that have been completed but not yet sold to customers.

first-stage allocation. The process through which manufacturing overhead costs are assigned to activity cost pools in an activity-based costing system.

fixed cost. A cost that remains constant in total, within a relevant range, even as activity changes. On a per unit basis, it varies inversely with changes in activity.

flexible budget. A budget that has been designed to cover a range of activity and that can be used to develop budgeted costs at any point within that range to compare to actual costs incurred.

free cash flow. The amount of cash available from operations after adjusting for capital expenditures and cash dividends paid; calculated by subtracting capital expenditures and cash dividends paid from operating cash flow.

horizontal analysis. A technique for evaluating a series of financial statement data over a period of time to determine the increase or decrease that has taken place, expressed as either an amount or a percentage.

ideal standards. Standards in a standard costing system that allow for no machine breakdowns or other work interruptions and that require peak efficiency at all times.

incremental cost. Any change in cost between two alternative courses of action under consideration.

incremental revenue. Any change in revenue between two alternative courses of action under consideration.

indirect cost. Any cost that cannot be easily and conveniently traced to a specified cost object.

indirect labour. Labour costs of janitors, supervisors, materials handlers, and other factory workers that cannot be conveniently and easily traced to individual units of product.

indirect materials. Materials costs for small items such as glue and nails that are an integral part of a finished product but cannot be conveniently and easily traced to individual units of product.

intellectual capital. Comprised of human capital (knowledge, skills, and experience), relational capital (external relationships including customers and suppliers), and structural capital (knowledge that remains within the entity and includes procedures and systems).

internal control. The entire system of controls, both financial and nonfinancial, established in order to provide reasonable assurance of effective and efficient operation, internal financial control, and compliance with laws and regulations.

internal rate of return. The rate or return promised by a capital investment project over its useful life. It is the discount rate at which the present value of all cash inflows exactly equals the present value of all cash outflows so that the net present value is zero.

inventory turnover ratio. A liquidity measure that shows the number of times on average that inventory is sold during the period; calculated by dividing cost of goods sold by the average inventory during the period.

investment centre. A business segment whose manager has control over costs, revenues, and invested funds.

joint cost. Any cost incurred up to the split-off point in a process that produces joint products.

joint products. Two or more items that are produced using a common input.

just-in-time (JIT). A production and inventory control system where raw materials are purchased and units of output are produced only on an as-needed basis to meet customer demand.

keep or drop decision. Decision resulting from a relevant cost analysis concerning whether a product line or segment should be retained or dropped.

knowledge management. A collective phrase for a series of processes and practices used by organisations in order to increase their value by improving the effectiveness of the generation and application of intellectual capital.

liquidity. The ability of a company to pay its short-term obligations as they are expected to become due within the next year or operating cycle.

liquidity ratios. Measures of the company's ability to pay its short-term obligations as they become due and to meet unexpected needs for cash as they arise.

make or buy decision. Decision resulting from a relevant cost analysis concerning whether an item should be produced internally or purchased from an outside source.

management by exception. A system of management that involves setting standards for various operating activities and then comparing actual results to these standards, with any significant differences being brought to the attention of management as "exceptions."

managerial accounting. Accounting activities concerned with providing information to managers for planning and control purposes and for making operating decisions.

manufacturing overhead. Any manufacturing cost that cannot be classified as direct labour or direct materials.

manufacturing overhead budget. A detailed plan that shows all production costs except direct materials and direct labour that are expected to be incurred over a specified time period.

marketing or selling costs. Any cost associated with securing customer orders and delivering the finished product or service into the hands of the customer.

master budget. A summary of the organisation's plans in which specific targets are set for sales, production, distribution, and financing activities; generally includes a cash budget, budgeted income statement, and budgeted balance sheet.

merchandise purchases budget. A detailed plan that shows the amount of goods a merchandising company must purchase from suppliers during the period in order to cover projected sales and provide desired levels of ending inventory.

mission and vision statements. Statements that aim to describe the purpose of an organisation, define its success, outline its strategy, and share its values.

mixed cost. A cost that contains both fixed and variable elements.

net operating income. Income before interest and income taxes have been deducted.

net present value. The difference between the present value of all cash inflows and the present value of all cash outflows associated with a capital investment project.

operating assets. Cash, accounts receivable, inventory, plant and equipment, and any other assets held for productive use by an organisation.

operating department. Any department or segment within an organisation within which the central purposes of the organisation are carried out.

operating lease. An agreement allowing one party (the lessee) to use the asset of another party (the lessor) in an arrangement accounted for as a rental.

opportunity cost. The potential benefit that is foregone when one alternative is selected over another.

outsourcing. The use of external suppliers as a source of finished products, components, or services. Also known as contract manufacturing or subcontracting.

payback period. The length of time that it takes for a capital investment project to fully recover its initial cash outflows from the cash inflows that it generates.

performance report. A detailed report that compares budgeted data with actual results.

period cost. Any cost that is reported on the income statement in the period in which it is incurred or accrued; such costs consist of marketing and administrative expenses.

planning. Selecting a course of action and specifying how it will be implemented.

planning and control cycle. The flow of management activities through planning, directing and motivating, controlling, and then back to planning again.

post audit. The follow-up that occurs after a capital investment project has been approved and implemented to determine whether expected results are actually realised.

practical standards. Standards in a standard costing system that allow for ordinary machine downtime and other work interruptions, and which can be attained through the reasonable but highly efficient efforts by the average worker.

predictive accounting. The use of process information to project future financial and nonfinancial performance.

present value. The value today of an amount to be received at some future date after taking current interest rates into account.

prime cost. Cost of the inputs to the production process. It is the sum of direct materials costs plus direct labour costs.

process reengineering. Improving operations by completely redesigning business processes in order to eliminate unnecessary steps, minimise errors, and reduce costs.

product cost. Any cost associated with the purchase or manufacture of goods; not reported on the income statement until the period in which the finished product is sold; such costs consist of direct materials, direct labour, and manufacturing overhead.

production budget. A detailed plan that shows the number of units that must to be produced during a period in order to cover projected sales and provide desired levels of ending inventory.

profit centre. A business segment whose manager has control over costs and revenues but not over invested funds.

profit margin ratio. A measure of profitability that shows the percentage of each sales dollar that flows through to net income; calculated as net operating income divided by net sales.

profitability index. The ratio of the present value of a capital investment project's cash inflows to the present value of its cash outflows.

profitability ratios. Measures of the income or operating success of a company over a given period of time, usually one year.

quality of earnings. Refers to the level of full and transparent information that is provided to external users of a company's financial statements.

ratio. An expression of the mathematical relationship between two or more financial statement items that may be expressed as a percentage, a rate, or a proportion.

ratio analysis. A technique for evaluating financial statements that expresses the relationship among two or more selected financial statement items.

raw materials. Materials that are used to manufacture a finished product.

reciprocal allocation method. A method of allocating service department costs to operating departments that gives full recognition to interdepartmental services.

required rate of return. The minimum rate of return that any capital investment project must yield in order for it to be considered acceptable.

residual income. The net operating income of an investment centre that exceeds its minimum required return on operating assets.

responsibility accounting. An accountability system under which managers are held responsible for differences between budgeted and actual results only for those items of revenue and expense over which they can exert significant control.

responsibility centre. Any business segment whose manager has control over cost, revenue, invested funds, or all three.

return on equity. A measure of profitability that shows the efficiency with which operating assets were used to generate returns to stockholders; can be calculated by dividing net operating income by average common stockholders' funds.

return on investment (ROI). A measure of profitability that shows the efficiency with which operating assets were used to generate operating profits; can be calculated by dividing net operating income by average operating assets or by multiplying profit margin by asset turnover rate.

sales budget. A detailed schedule that shows the expected sales for coming periods, typically expressed both in dollars and in units.

second-stage allocation. The process by which activity rates are used to apply costs to products and customers in activity-based costing.

segment. Any part of an organisation that can be evaluated independently of other parts and about which management seeks financial data.

segment margin. The amount remaining after a segment's traceable fixed costs have been subtracted from its contribution margin. It represents the amount available after a segment has covered all of its own traceable costs.

sell or process further decision. Decision resulting from a relevant cost analysis concerning whether a joint product should be sold at the split-off point or sold after further processing.

selling and administrative expense budget. A detailed plan that shows the expected selling and administrative expenses that will be incurred during a specified period of time.

service department. Any department that provides support or assistance to operating departments but does not directly engage in production or other operating activities.

simple rate of return. The rate of a return on a capital investment project that is determined by dividing its annual accounting net operating income by the initial investment required. Also referred to as accounting rate of return.

solvency. The ability of a company to pay interest as it comes due and to repay the principal amount of a debt at its maturity.

solvency ratios. Measures of the ability of a company to pay its long-term obligations as they become due and to survive over time.

special order. Any one-time order that is not considered part of the organisation's ordinary on-going business.

split-off point. The point in the manufacturing process where some or all of the joint products can be recognised and sold as individual products.

static budget. A budget created prior to the onset of the budgeting period that is valid only for the planned activity level.

step allocation method. A method of allocating service department costs to operating departments that allocates service department costs to other service departments as well as to operating departments in a sequential fashion that typically starts with the service department that provides the greatest amount of service to other departments.

strategic enterprise management. An approach to strategic management that focuses on creating and sustaining shareholder value through the integrated use of best practice modelling and analysis techniques, technologies, and processes in support of better decision-making.

strategic planning. The formulation, evaluation, and selection of strategies for the purpose of preparing a long-term plan of action in order to attain objectives.

sunk cost. Any cost that has already been incurred or that cannot be changed by any decision made currently or in the future.

theory of constraints. A management approach that emphasises the importance of managing bottlenecks caused by scarce resources.

times interest earned ratio. A solvency measure of the company's ability to meet interest payments as they come due that can be calculated by dividing income before interest expense and income taxes by interest expense.

total manufacturing cost. Cost of all inputs to the production process during a period. It is the sum of direct materials used, direct labour incurred, and manufacturing overhead.

total quality management. An integrated and comprehensive system of planning and controlling all business functions so that products and services are produced that meet or exceed customer expectations.

traceable fixed cost. Any fixed cost that is incurred because of the existence of a particular business segment.

transaction driver. In activity-based costing, a simple count of the number of times an activity occurs.

treasury management. The corporate handling of all financial managers, the generation of internal and external funds for the business, the management of currencies and cash flows, and the complex strategies, policies, and procedures of corporate finance.

value chain. The major business functions that add value to an organisation's products or services, such as research and development, product design, manufacturing, marketing, distribution, and customer service.

value-based management. The process of searching for and implementing those activities that will contribute most to increases in shareholder value.

variable cost. A cost that varies in total, within a relevant range, in direct proportion to changes in activity. On a per unit basis, it remains constant as activity levels change.

variable cost ratio. The ratio of total variable costs to total revenues, or the ratio of unit variable cost to unit selling price. It is used in cost-volume-profit analysis.

variable costing. A costing method that treats only the variable manufacturing costs (direct materials, direct labour, and variable overhead) as product costs while it treats fixed overhead as a period cost. It is also referred to as direct costing.

vertical analysis. A technique for evaluating financial statement data that expresses each item in a financial statement as a per cent of a base amount.

work in process. Units of product that have been only partially completed and will require further work before they are ready for sale to customers.

working capital (net). A measure used to evaluate a company's liquidity and short-term debt-paying ability that can be calculated by subtracting total current liabilities from total current assets.

XBRL. A computer language for financial reporting known as eXtensible Business Reporting Language. It allows companies to publish, extract, and exchange financial information through the Internet and other electronic means in a standardised manner.

zero-based budget. A method of budgeting that requires managers each year to justify all costs as if the programmes involved were being proposed for the first time.

Printed in the United States
By Bookmasters